earth pledge

Promoting Sustainability Since 1991

Earth Pledge is a 501(c)(3) not for profit organization. Our mission is to identify and promote innovative techniques and technologies that restore the balance between human and natural systems. Through demonstration, education, and research, we deliver viable models to government, industry, and communities. The New York region is our laboratory for implementing replicable solutions that will inspire and facilitate a global transition to sustainability.

D0974293

Sustainable Architecture White Papers are part of the
Earth Pledge Series on Sustainable Development.

Earth Pledge
122 East 38th Street, New York, NY 10016.
Telephone (212) 725-6611
www.earthpledge.org

President: Theodore W. Kheel

Executive Director: Leslie Hoffman

Editors: David E. Brown, Mindy Fox, Mary Rickel Pelletier

Design: Kristen Kiger, Laurie Kaufman, Julia Reich

Printed using vegetable ink on chlorine-free, FSC-certified, 30%
post consumer waste recycled paper for cover and text.

ISBN 0-9675099-1-2

TABLE OF CONTENTS

i

SECTION 2: BUILDING COMMUNITY

SECTION 3: PUBLIC WORKS

SECTION 6: RESOURCES

Introduction

Leslie Hoffman, Executive Director
Earth Pledge

This third volume in a series of white papers published by Earth Pledge continues a tradition that began in eighteenth-century England, where white papers provided a forum for important social and political issues. Our first collection, on sustainable cities, was a contribution to the United Nations Conference on Human Settlements in Istanbul in June 1996. Our *Sustainable Cuisine White Papers* followed in April 1999, and now we offer these readings on sustainable architecture.

Sustainable architecture has deep and personal roots for me. As a student of architecture and design in college, I connected with shelter as a basic human need. I worked for the college cabinetmaker during my studies, and later became a contractor in Maine. I focused on energy and resource efficiency, and while running my own construction company I collaborated with engineers and architects to incorporate and promote sustainability while building new buildings and renovating old ones.

Earth Pledge's offices are housed in WorkSpace, an environmental and communications technology showcase. Made possible by the support of our many sponsors, this "old made new" building is a great tool to promote the concepts and ideals discussed in this book.

Many of the tenets of sustainability are old ideas. Some are ancient understandings, others are developments of the last decades. The writings here are by those who have recognized the need to promote sustainability in architecture and its related disciplines. We owe them thanks for persevering. It is uplifting to see the mainstream of these trades finally beginning to adopt sustainable practices.

There are two well-worn sayings that have fresh relevance for this book: Good ideas come from all kinds of places, and You are either part of the problem or part of the solution. The authors of the papers you are about to read are people who, regardless of the role they play in relation to our habitats, are leading us towards a more sustainable future. Please join them and the many others who are moving in the right direction.

Preface

Paul Hawken, Author

Architecture was once, literally, the study and knowledge of arches. Of course it was more than that, but a strong arch and a long-lasting building were virtually synonymous. Unless the flying buttresses, vaulted ceilings, apses, and entries were perfectly designed, in perfect accord with the fundamental geometry of architecture, a building wouldn't last. Today, the discipline has come back to the circle, not a circle of stone but rather the cyclical principles of nature and human endeavor.

As we know too well, modern buildings are temporal in every sense. In many contemporary houses, construction quality is barely better than that of a theater set. Materials are made to fade, not to last. It is as if the weltanschauung of Nathanael West's famous deconstruction of Los Angeles, *The Day of the Locust*, had become national policy. The impact of this shoddiness is equally degrading to people and the environment.

Sustainable architecture is foremost about reimagining the relationship between human beings and living systems. The most powerful expression of this relationship is our built environment. How do we build now that there are six billion of us, now that our supply of natural capital—water, wood, energy, land—must be far more effectively used? How do we make zero-emission houses? How do we design structures that can be reincorporated into the earth harmlessly and endlessly? How do we metabolize energy and water so that the sky and land improve rather than erode? In other words, given how many we are and how much we have come to expect, how do we live?

Architecture in its traditional role is probably a dying profession. Today, architects must work with systems; they must design new ways of living and working in which buildings play a key role. We desperately need mediators between human need and the enduring cycles of nature. Architects can, and must, inhabit this new role.

This book is imbued with the voices of the new leaders, the pioneers. They will be famous a hundred years from now for their courage and vision. Today, they are absolutely necessary if we are to continue our life on earth. They need to be listened to, and honored, just as they ask us to listen to the natural world and honor it.

SECTION 1:

PRACTICE

Eco-Effectiveness:
A New Design
Strategy

William McDonough,
Co-founder and CEO of McDonough
Braungart Design Chemistry and
Principal at William McDonough + Partners

Dr. Michael Braungart,
Co-founder and Chairman of McDonough
Braungart Design Chemistry

William McDonough + Partners and
McDonough Braungart Design Chemistry, LLC
410 East Water Street, Suite 500
Charlottesville, VA 22902
www.mcdonough.com
www.mbdc.com

In *The Effective Executive*, Peter Drucker describes such a business leader as someone who is doing the right thing. It might seem easy to transfer this advice to sustainable architecture and design. The right thing must be to make buildings and systems that pollute, contaminate, and deplete less than their predecessors do, right? But in doing that we simply become more efficient at the wrong thing. And in letting us think that we are achieving environmental progress, this strategy might be even more pernicious. We must instead start with a more difficult question: What *is* the right thing?

Our answer is eco-effectiveness. Eco-effectiveness is a broad strategy, not just an ecological one. It engages the idea of an effective economy producing profits for companies in the business of making profits, while treating people fairly and well and respecting, even celebrating, the natural world. This goes beyond a more conventional single-issue approach, which might focus, for example, on social responsibility or energy efficiency.

The current architectural paradigm produces houses that are machines for living in, office buildings that are machines for working in, and churches that are machines for praying in. Buildings end up with sealed, tinted windows that minimize the amount of daylight coming in to cut heat gain. Their air-conditioning systems provide little fresh air. This building type has been designed more for the efficiency of its operations (that is, its machines) than for the people inside. In other words, it is a work support system for people who don't, it seems, have a life. Such design can be seen as timefully mindless: it is done in a hurry and it is mindless of its effects, both physical and psychological, on the human beings who use the building. It is mindless, as well, of its effects on the larger planetary system—on the forests, water and air quality, species abundance, soil health, and so on.

When faced with this current state of architecture, designers must understand that being less bad (or more efficient) is not necessarily being good. Eco-effectiveness recognizes this crucial point. So what then does it mean to be good, to do the right thing?

How about designing a building that nourishes and restores living systems? That engages propitiously with the industrial system in a way that does not destroy nature? Imagine a structure that is actually fecund, providing more to the environment than it takes away; that engages with the sun the way a tree does, with a photosynthetic connection, moisture transpiration, habitation by hundreds of species, transformation of microclimate, distillation of water, and production of complex sugars and carbohydrates; that sequesters carbon, fixes nitrogen, and changes with the seasons. Imagine a building like a tree, a city like a forest.

Eco-effective design requires a reconsideration of the very concept of high technology. How many modern designs are as elegant and sophisticated as a tree? How many buildings have humans designed that produce oxygen? Is a high-tech building one that destroys air quality, or enhances it?

William McDonough + Partners designs buildings that attempt to achieve these goals. A building we designed for The Gap in San Bruno, California, features an undulating meadow of grasses on its roof to invite songbirds back to the site, to absorb stormwater, and to provide a delightful environment for the inhabitants of the area. A building we designed for Oberlin College in Ohio will generate more energy than it needs to operate—in effect paying back its energy mortgage—and is modeled on fecund and generative natural systems.

McDonough Braungart Design Chemistry is designing products that do not follow the traditional produce/use/discard model. Instead, they are "products of service": customers buy products' services, not their materials. Take industrial carpet, for example. Customers use our carpet for as long as they need it or as long as it lasts. When it is time for replacement, the carpet is returned to the manufacturer for true recycling. (Most conventional recycling is actually "downcycling," which reduces a material's quality and its potential uses over time.) We are also designing fabrics that, when they abrade in normal use, are safe to breathe in, rather than using materials that can fill indoor air with toxins.

Architecture can be a healing act. We look forward to a time when products and buildings are designed as nutrients, of office buildings full of daylight and fresh air that send you home refreshed, of houses that feel like natural extensions of place and psyche. These are rich agendas, not simply the technological and stylistic gloss of current fashion.

From the level of the molecule to that of the region, design can be utterly transforming. It can, in fact, move humans from a strategy of tragedy to a strategy of change. These strategies of change allow for healthy, beautiful, profitable products and systems. But first, designers must fiercely confront the important questions of their day. We believe one of the most important questions in this age is, How do we love all the children, of all species, for all time? Not just some of the children, but all of the children. With such a question in mind, it is easy to understand the tremendous, transforming power of good design.

———— ∞∞∞ ————

Solar Electric Buildings

Steven J. Strong, President

Solar Design Associates, Inc.
P.O. Box 242
Harvard, MA 01451
www.solardesign.com

The last two decades have brought significant changes to the design profession. In the wake of traumatic escalations in energy prices, oil shortages, embargoes, and war, along with heightened concerns over pollution, environmental degradation, and resource depletion, awareness of the environmental impact of our work as design professionals has dramatically increased. The shortcomings of yesterday's buildings have also become increasingly clear: inefficient electrical and climate conditioning systems squander great amounts of energy; combustion of fossil fuels on-site and at power plants adds greenhouse gasses, acid rain, and other pollutants to the environment; many building materials, furnishings, and finishes give off toxic by-products contributing to indoor air pollution;

and poorly designed lighting and ventilation systems can induce headaches and fatigue.

Architects with vision have come to understand that good design must respond to aesthetic values as well as environmental concerns. These architects have responded by specifying increased levels of thermal insulation, healthier interiors, higher-efficiency lighting, better glazings and HVAC equipment, air-to-air heat exchangers, and heat-recovery ventilation systems, among other technologically progressive equipment. This is all an important first step, but it is not enough. For developed countries to continue to enjoy the comforts of the late twentieth century and for the developing world to ever hope to attain them, sustainability must become the cornerstone of our design philosophy. Rather then using less nonrenewable fuels and creating less pollution, we must design buildings that produce some, and eventually all, of their own energy, and create no pollution.

Every building being designed today that relies on fossil fuel will become obsolete before its projected lifetime is over. Oil industry analysts expect world oil extraction to peak within the next five to 10 years. After that, we will begin the long and irreversible downward slide as demand greatly exceeds supply and prices escalate. Burning oil for its thermal content will no longer be economically justified.

As the era of cheap oil draws to a close, we must begin in earnest to develop other energy sources.

One of the most promising renewable energy technologies is photovoltaics. Photovoltaics (PV) is a truly elegant means of producing electricity on site, directly from the sun, without concern for energy supply or environmental harm. These solid-state devices simply make electricity out of sunlight, silently and with no maintenance, no pollution, and no depletion of materials.

There is a growing consensus that the first solar electric systems to reach widespread commercialization will be building-integrated PV (BIPV) systems, where PV elements actually become an integral part of the building. Architects in Europe, Japan, and the United States are now beginning to explore innovative ways of incorporating such systems into their designs. Manufacturers are responding with PV modules specifically designed for building-integrated applications, including integral roof modules, roofing tiles and shingles, and modules for vertical curtain wall facades, sunshades, sloped glazing systems, and skylights.

Building-integrated PV systems offer several benefits. First, the infrastructure is already in place: Building owners are already paying for facade and/or roofing materials and the labor to install them. The land is already paid for, the site work is already complete, the support structure is already in place, the building is already wired, the utility is already connected, and developers can finance the PV as part of their overall project. When BIPV installations are spread over a very broad geographic area and a large number of buildings, the effects of local weather conditions are reduced, making the power supply resilient and consistent. Well-integrated PV systems are architecturally "clean," increasing their acceptance by clients and the public. And a BIPV system provides building owners with a highly visible public expression of their environmental commitment.

The Carlisle House in Carlisle, Massachusetts, designed by Solar Design Associates and completed in 1980, was the first residential application of a BIPV system. Built in conjunction with MIT and the Department of Energy, this all-electric house burns no fossil fuel on-site and generates a surplus of electricity exported to the local utility grid. Other projects in the United States followed, including the 200 kWp (kilowatt-peak) Solarex facility in Frederick, Maryland (1982), and the 325 kWp Georgetown University Intercultural Center in Washington, D.C. (1985). Aggressive efforts to adopt BIPV began in Europe and Japan in the early 1990s and have pushed the technology toward broader commercial acceptance.

But BIPV systems are only a part of the whole building solution. In designing with BIPV, it is essential to appreciate the context within which solar electricity can best function. We must also address both sides of the energy-use equation—supply and consumption. To maximize the solar contribution, a building should be designed to use energy as efficiently as possible.

A building's energy efficiency comes from the materials and processes with which it is constructed. A high-integrity thermal envelope with monolithic air and moisture barriers and superior, high-R-value glazing is important. Passive solar strategies that reduce heating and cooling requirements should be employed along with daylighting and energy-efficient equipment and systems. Solar thermal systems should be considered for space and water heating. Advanced mechanical systems such as heat-recovery ventilation and geothermal heat pumps can increase energy efficiency.

In the past, incorporating PV into a building design required concessions during the design process. Today, as PV manufacturers match products to building-industry standards and architects' requirements, this is changing. These companies are actively pursuing new PV modules that displace conventional building materials. "Custom color" crystalline solar cells are also being introduced in order to add aesthetic variety to BIPV systems. Other architectural modules employ glass-superstrate, crystalline modules with space between the cells and translucent backings to provide diffuse daylighting along with electric production. A number of companies are making PV elements in unique sizes and shapes, with custom cell sizes and spacings; insulated PV roofing systems for flat roofs; modules that replace conventional view and spandrel glass; and PV tiles for sloped-roof applications.

These new building-integrated photovoltaic components are providing a window into the future of solar architecture. With the right design, the sunlight falling on a building can provide much or all of the power it requires. In urban areas, one can only imagine the power that will be generated by incorporating PV into the thousands of square miles of flat, empty roofs and other available building surfaces that receive generous amounts of sunlight.

In only two decades, PV has moved from the research laboratory to professional applications. The technology is now ready for widespread commercialization. As architects and building engineers become involved in its design, PV technology is taking a more sophisticated, elegant, and appropriate role in architeccture. As building-integrated PV components become an integral part of the form and aesthetic of the built environment, these systems will contribute greatly to a more sustainable future for their owners, their communities, and society at large.

The Art of Architecture in the Age of Ecology

James Wines, President and Founder of SITE,
Head of the Department of Architecture
at Pennsylvania State University

SITE Environmental Design
25 Maiden Lane, 2nd Floor
New York, NY 10038
www.siteenvirodesign.com

"The 'control of nature' is a phrase conceived in arrogance, born of the Neanderthal age of biology and the convenience of Man."

—*Rachel Carson*

This is potentially one of the most challenging periods of architectural innovation in history. While many of the established architects today seem intimidated by the accelerating momentum of change—fearing their stylistic commitments may be under attack—there is no reason why the environmental revolution cannot be welcomed as the threshold of a great creative era. Here is an opportunity to invent the future on terms that are sociologically and ecologically responsible.

The quest for a conceptually liberating approach in architecture, leading to the inclusion and trans-formation of environmental content, will have to start with a questioning of the profession's insular ideologies and xenophobic tendencies to resist new ideas. The first of these questionable shibboleths would have to be the assumption that architecture is an obligatory orchestration of massive sculptural volumes. Obviously any building is a composition of physical elements; but this does not have to be seen as an interpretive bias. More often than not Industrial Age design conventions fail to address issues of human scale and the pedestrian's psychological need for the reduction of large vertical planes into a readable level of detail. Certainly the primary lesson of Medieval and Renaissance architecture in Europe is the powerful artistic value of sculptural ornamen-tation, light- and shadow-capturing surfaces, and iconographic legibility in buildings and public spaces.

The fundamental urban design flaw of the twentieth century has been the tendency of architects to assume that abstract formal exercises shrunken to tabletop models—however seductive as Lilliputian artifacts —would automatically convert to a comprehensible scale when actually built. The relentless bleakness and oppressive gigantism of the contemporary cityscape are ample testimony to these misguided indulgences. In contrast, the profusion of evocative subject matter associated with nature, its comfortable scale relationships to the human body, the complexity of its structure, and the science of describing its processes offer a vast reservoir of ideas and imagery for infusing architecture with a more relevant visual content.

The reliance of designers on tabletop design is especially problematic now, since it is exacerbated by computer-aided-design technology. It opens up architecture to an aesthetically revealing evaluation that might be described as "the pedestal test." This means of critique acknowledges that a great deal of current architecture is derived from Cubist and Constructivist sculptural forms that are usually considered old-fashioned when appraised in an art context, but enthusiastically embraced by various contemporary architects as a source of emancipation. The pedestal test proposes that good buildings in model form—especially those with declared environmental ambitions—can be weeded out from the bad examples based on whether they look more convincing on their intended construction sites or on exhibition plinths. By these standards, there is an inherent risk that an extreme example of bombastic and convoluted shape-making for its own sake (with the inevitable intrusion of these conceits on functional space) frequently comes closer to being classified as mediocre sculpture than progressive architecture. It could be postulated that any artifact that is visually improved by its presentation on a pedestal simply reinforces its limited state of "objectness." If a building at the model stage looks better on a base, there is a good chance it should probably stay there.

Sustainable architecture basically comes down to three purposes—first, to advance the purely selfish motive of survival by a cooperation with nature; second, to build shelter in concert with ecological principles as part of this objective; and third, to address the deeper philosophical conflicts surrounding the issue of whether we really deserve the luxury of this existence, given our appalling track record of environmental abuse.

But a further, and ultimate, question remains: If we convince ourselves that we really merit nature's blessings, what does the notion of sustainability have to do with the soul and the concept of a spiritual eternity? The philosophy of sustainability is associated with various past societies' perception of eternity. It has been inseparable from historic architecture ever since early religious connections were made between the concept of an "everlasting soul," the need to honor this spirit by offering provisional housing en route to paradise, and the construction of awesome monumental sanctuaries to symbolize the mission (as in ancient Egypt). In today's world, there doesn't seem to be much call for architecture as a spiritual depot. Religions now exert far less ritual power over the mass of people than, for example, Catholicism imposed during the twelfth century, and they have lost a great deal of theological credibility to the more persuasive picture of eternity described by science.

One of the most disturbing paradoxes that emerges from studying humanity's relation to the environment gnaws at the roots of cultural and theological development since the birth of the world's dominant religions. Aboriginal cultures see their relationship to nature as part of a single harmonious continuum. Spiritually, this is achieved through a hierarchy of totems that connect to their ancestral origins, a cosmology that places them at one with the environment, and behavior patterns that respect ecological balance. At the opposite philosophical extreme, contemporary technocracies perceive of nature as a foe to be challenged and as an unwanted impediment to progress.

How are we to reconcile the environmental success of so many multitheistic ancient and Aboriginal civilizations—where each element of nature was identified by its own divine spirit—versus the dominant monotheism of today, where an all-embracing (male) God is proclaimed in the human image and the destruction of the Earth is viewed as a privilege of Man's sovereignty in the universe? There is substantial evidence that a distribution of responsibility among multiple gods (of both male and female gender) related to the sun, rain, soil, rivers, crops, etc., has been a far more productive theological vision, both ecologically and agriculturally, than the despotic egocentrism associated with a single deity and the myopic delusions of "nature for Man's convenience."

This anthropocentric concept of Man at the center of the universe and the parallel manufacture of deities forged in the human image grew out of the luxury of an extended period of relative atmospheric and geological stability. These idyllic conditions have reinforced the conceit that nature exists for our convenience. This vision has undergone an infinite number of definitions and revisions throughout history; but the underlying theme has remained relatively constant, producing such extremes of environmental success and failure as civilizations that scripted their own demise in less than a few decades to others that endured for thousands of years.

As we enter the new millennium, architecture has one primary mission—to progress from ego-centric to eco-centric. This evolution refers to a mental state of transference where the habitual notions of an insulated psyche (detached from ecological awareness) are exchanged for the reawakening of an expansive sense of "oneness" with nature. Depending on the strength of its Earth-centric philosophy (or relative fear of nature's revenge), each past civilization seems to have risen and fallen based on its capacity to achieve a balance with the natural environment. It is a history without logical chronology or rational structure. The only consistent pattern seems to be a repeated scenario where the most exploitative cultures invariably committed some form of environmental suicide. Our confused ecological policies today are simply a legacy of these ancient priority systems, complicated by the unprecedented growth of a conquer-the-Earth mentality and its delusion of absolute sovereignty over nature. Whatever the ecclesiastical prescriptions and fears of divine reprisal that kept earlier societies in check, these restraints have all but disappeared.

Nature is primal, metamorphic, and endlessly ambiguous. It is rich in associations and the one totally universal source of ideas and symbolism in the arts. It is a genesis of communicative content that strips away redundancies and constantly reveals new information. Through its infinite complexity, nature is an instructive and inspirational influence that can expand the aesthetic horizons of the building arts and confirm the inalienable right of humanity to try to salvage a place on this planet before it's too late. The mission now in architecture, as in all human endeavor, is to recover those fragile threads of connectedness with nature that have been lost for most of this century. The key to a truly sustainable art of architecture for the new millennium will depend on the creation of bridges that unite conservation technology with an Earth-centric philosophy and the capacity of designers to transform these integrated forces into a new visual language.

This essay was adapted from James Wines, *The Art of Architecture in the Age of Ecology* (Taschen, 1998).

Landscapes that Renew

Diana Balmori, Principal

Balmori Associates, Inc.
129 Church Street, Suite 304
New Haven, CT 06510
www.balmori.com

Twenty years ago, a new awareness of ecology made our office look at the ways landscapes were affected by the different things done *to* them, especially air and water pollution. Today we think of the landscape in a much more active way, as a live agent capable of changing the surrounding conditions, for better or for worse. Our role as designers therefore is to design landscapes that can thrive in and improve those conditions. I'll give two examples, which both happen to be new types of landscapes. One is the linear park, or greenway. The other is the roof garden.

Greenways are the twenty-first-century park par excellence. Their implications are dramatic: for a relatively small amount of money, these narrow green corridors can reconnect parts of a city. They can weave themselves through a city, spreading themselves democratically to reach all areas. They can be attached to streams, rivers, or shores to provide soft edges and restore flood plains. And they function as pathways for people to travel using their own exertions, not as ancillaries to an avenue of cars. Though the idea of the greenway is less than 15 years old, it has the potential to mobilize our life in cities, introducing pedestrian movement areas and acting as "green lungs."

There are many other positive effects of greenways. They encourage people to use their feet again. They can foster a community of businesses along their edges, so that we might once again be able to get a loaf of bread or a bottle of aspirin by walking or biking or skating. They can also provide critical migration corridors for animals through urban areas. They are active landscapes, which can introduce open, green space to various parts of the city; intensify topographic features, rivers, ridges; offer a soft surface capable of absorbing rainwater; and let people escape the car-dominated hardscape.

The transformative power of greenways comes from the connections they are capable of producing. Up to now, greenways have developed without arms, as straight 10- to 15-foot-wide strips wherever their right-of-way was plunked: an abandoned railway, the side of a river, a utility corridor. But they can link to this museum, to that bakery, to the marathon, to the concert, to the state park, to the political speech, be it as a permanent path or as a temporary one-day street closure. This modest caterpillar with the possibility of becoming a centipede is a landscape that can actively change a community: greening, invigorating, and connecting.

The roof garden is a landscape not yet established, but it is one that could truly change a city both for individuals and as a whole. Although individuals would have to create them independently, the sum effect of hundreds or thousands of modest roof gardens atop individual buildings would be to reduce a city's "heat island" effect; help dispose urban run off from storms; and establish many small, personally pleasurable oases in a landscape usually dominated by hot, tarred surfaces.

With their black tar roofs constantly exposed to the sun, cities soak up great amounts of heat, increasing temperatures both day and night, as that stored heat is slowly released after sunset. High urban temperatures also worsen smog conditions. Roof gardens can give shade while their plants absorb carbon dioxide and put oxygen in the air and cool a city down. The shade of a single tree with a 15-foot canopy can lower the temperature under it by three to four degrees Fahrenheit. This cooling can become even greater as moisture is released by evaporation into the surrounding atmosphere. And the cooling effect is further enhanced when the leaves cool down at night, which allows them to absorb more heat the next day. Computer models created by the Lawrence Berkeley National Laboratory in California show that a city with hundreds of roof gardens could reduce the urban temperature by as much as five degrees Fahrenheit. Germany and France already provide incentives for creating roof gardens; closer to home, Seattle is considering such a move as a simpler and cheaper solution for disposing of urban run off. In Chicago, Mayor Daley is devoting $1 million to an experimental rooftop garden atop City Hall.

The large acreage of a city makes the disposal of rainwater a problem during heavy storms. Urban drainage systems channel all this rainwater into pipes and dump it into whatever urban streams and rivers are at hand. The sudden rush of enormous volumes of water at great speed pulls pollution off the paved surfaces, through drainage pipes, and into rivers. And as a river's volume increases, the water's speed multiplies and the banks of the river are eroded, vegetation is torn from its sides, and banks are flooded. The more a city builds over open land, the more water it must dispose of. Volume thus grows, as do the size and cost of the drainage system and the devastating effects on the rivers and streams that receive all the water.

By contrast, when rainwater falls on an unpaved, non-urban site it is absorbed. A planted surface stabilized by roots, stalks, trees, and composted material breaks the impact of the falling water, slows it, and gives it someplace to go. Though some water will run off, it will move slowly. Some of this water returns to the atmosphere through evapotranspiration, some trickles through the earth into the water table (being filtered as it moves), some runs off into rivers and streams.

Roof gardens can achieve many of these same things (though there is no route from a roof to the water table). The more rooftop plantings there are, the less water reaches the paved ground, storm drains, and beleaguered urban rivers. The greener rooftops are, the less heat is absorbed (and released) by a city. And roof gardens also create attractive, healthy environments where once there was only hot, tarred roofs.

Greenways and rooftops are very different landscapes. One is a large-scale urban intervention, existing on the ground for everyone to use. The other is an individual act, the transformation of one piece of private property into a green space. Yet both are active landscapes, with the potential to transform our cities by regenerating natural cycles within an urban fabric that has lost them. Ultimately, this makes for healthier cities and healthier people.

———◦◦◦———

Living Buildings

Jason Frederick McLennan, Director,
Elements, a division of BNIM

BNIM Architects
1200 Main Street, Suite 1515
Kansas City, MO 64105
www.bnim.com

A few years ago I was asked to give a talk in Northern California on the future of architecture. I had been asked because of work I was doing with Bob Berkebile, one of the pioneers of the green architecture movement, on a project at Montana State University that was partially funded by the National Institute of Standards and Technology. Berkebile had hired me to help him and a large team of scientists, engineers, and educators develop a prototype building for the twenty-first century.

The building, known as the EpiCenter, would combine emerging technologies with age-old strategies to generate less pollution than any conventional building, both in its construction and operation, while enhancing the productivity and creative synergy of the students and researchers that would inhabit it. We had been given the task of designing the future, or at least of showing what was possible if we dared to dream of a future where our buildings no longer took from the environment, but were restorative.

My role was to identify appropriate technologies and then help the design team weave these into the fabric of the EpiCenter—to integrate systems and close loops between them. My talk in California was timely, because it allowed me opportunity to reflect on the goals of the project and put them in a framework that could be easily described to an audience with varied backgrounds. In preparing the talk, I realized that what I needed most was not drawings and images of buildings, but a metaphor—a simple way to describe the future that would embody the principles I wished to communicate while conjuring up images that told a complete story.

Using metaphors to describe things can provide an astounding amount of clarity and allow us to understand complex systems quickly, but they can also lock us into set ways of thinking. For too long now the machine has been the primary metaphor for our buildings, which implies a relationship with nature that is exploitative and relies on brute force combined with great amounts of energy to solve problems. It is a nineteenth-century model that has been carried forth into the twenty-first century. With architecture, however, when the metaphor changes, new sets of rules emerge that can guide the design process.

While preparing for my speech I had time to stroll for a few hours on the beach, watching the waves roll in and out and feeling the abrasiveness of the crisp salt air on my skin and lungs. I found myself searching amidst the sand and rocks for this new metaphor, a metaphor that could replace the machine. Serendipity being the mother of all inventions, I soon came upon some tiny flowers eking out an existence in this harsh but beautiful climate. Growing in clumps in poor soil on the top of the primary sand dune, exposed to harsh, brackish water and sometimes at the mercy of gale-force winds, were several tiny bushes that sported beautiful purple flowers. Here was a thriving plant that not only had evolved perfectly to suit its environment, but also enriched it, retaining soil, providing habitat, and storing rainwater as needed. It was a perfect metaphor for the building of the future.

Flowers are marvels of adaptation, growing in various shapes, sizes, and forms. Some lie dormant through the harshest of winters only to emerge each spring once the ground has thawed. Others stay rooted year-round, opening and closing in response to changing conditions, such as the availability of sunlight. Like buildings, they are literally and figuratively rooted in place, able to draw resources only from the square inches of earth and sky that they inhabit. The flower must receive all of its energy from the sun, all of its water needs from the sky, and all of the nutrients necessary for survival from the soil. Flowers are also miniature ecosystems, supporting and sheltering microorganisms and insects like our buildings do for us. Equally important, flowers are beautiful and thus can provide the inspiration needed for architecture to truly be successful.

Bucky Fuller once said, "We do not seek to imitate nature, but rather to find the principles she uses." By following those basic principles we can imagine whole cities operating like complex ecosystems, processing water and waste while generating energy. The focus will change from region to region but a high level of environmental performance will be constant. Communities in desert regions will be designed to maximize their ability to collect water, and, like the plants of the desert, to retain and conserve that water. In colder climates the focus will shift to retaining heat and capturing the available sunlight.

After that walk I decided to call the future of architecture a future of living buildings. Like their flowering counterparts, living buildings operate from seven simple principles. Living buildings will:

- Harvest all their own water and energy needs on site.

- Be adapted specifically to site and climate and evolve as conditions change.

- Operate pollution-free and generate no wastes that aren't useful for some other process in the building or immediate environment.

- Promote the health and well-being of all inhabitants, as a healthy ecosystem does.

- Be comprised of integrated systems that maximize efficiency and comfort.

- Improve the health and diversity of the local ecosystem rather than degrade it.

- Be beautiful and inspire us to dream.

When I got back to the hotel I had my lecture ready as well as a fresh perspective on how to discuss design for the twenty-first century. The amazing thing is that we already have the technology necessary to create buildings that can perform like the living buildings I envisioned. From photovoltaics to fuel cells, the technology research we performed and applied at the EpiCenter shows that the future is available, if we only have the desire and foresight to accept it.

―∞∞∞―

Building Integrated Photovoltaics

Gregory Kiss, Principal

Kiss + Cathcart Architects
44 Court Street, 12th Floor
Brooklyn, NY 11201
www.kisscathcart.com

B uildings are the largest single consumer of electricity in the developed world. What if buildings produced energy instead of consuming it?

At Kiss + Cathcart, we have been working for the last 15 years to develop energy-producing building systems, with a focus on photovoltaics (PVs)—solid state modules that turn sunlight into electricity. We believe that PV energy-generating buildings and infrastructure are not only practical, but inevitable. Two crucial trends are converging: PV technologies are becoming more efficient, affordable, and reliable, and buildings are being designed to use less energy, reducing the size and cost of the PV systems needed. PVs have the added benefit of providing independence from commercial grid power, with its geographical constraints and variable costs. The distributed, decentralized future is already here in information technology, and soon will arrive in the energy sector.

The benefits of changing energy paradigms are virtually incalculable. Energy is the largest component of the world's economy, and is currently its worst polluter. Energy, particularly electricity, makes possible many of the essential elements of modern life, including communications, education, entertainment, and health care. More energy is urgently needed every-where in the world. Where will it come from? What will be the costs in pollution? And where will this energy go?

Electric generators are getting smaller and cheaper. Gas-fired power plants are yielding to microturbines —localized units that power a single house. Fuel cells that more efficiently convert gas or other fuels to electricity are becoming available. These small, modular power sources have many advantages, for both the overburdened power grids of the developed world and the embryonic infrastructure of the developing world. But they are all still based on burning fossil fuels. They require constant fuel supplies and significant maintenance, and emit carbon as an end product. Renewable technologies—wind power, hydroelectricity, and solar power—minimize these problems and, in some cases, eliminate them completely.

For years, the most economically sensible place to install solar-electric systems has been in remote sites at least a mile from a power line, where PV installations typically outperform other forms of electric generation or supply. Recently, though, stand-alone PV products such as streetlights, telephones, and parking meters have sprung up in cities and suburbs: it is often much less expensive to use freestanding PV equipment than to dig a new trench for wires.

On a larger scale, building-integrated PV—systems where PV modules serve as integral components of a structure—is becoming economically feasible due to progress in two critical areas: material flexibility and cost. State-of-the-art photovoltaic modules are thin layers of semiconductor material deposited on glass, sheet metal, or (in the near future) recycled plastics. These PV materials are very similar to many widely used building materials. For example, almost all glass used in construction today is coated with thin layers of metals to produce color, reflectivity, or improved insulating qualities. It is only a small leap to imagine mass-produced glass coated with PV materials. Also, PV modules are steadily approaching price parity with similar non-solar materials. Ten years ago the average cost of solar modules was over $60 per square foot. Today the lowest unsubsidized market price for photovoltaic panels is a little less than $10 per square foot—lower than stone, metal panels, and even high-end architectural glass.

Photovoltaic products have also developed in other important ways: they are available in larger sizes, in custom shapes and colors, as insulating roof units, as replacements for asphalt shingles, and as translucent or patterned glass for skylights and windows. So it is now practical, and increasingly economical, to make buildings from solar products. Why are there not more solar buildings? There are notable barriers remaining in established norms, such as building codes and the interests of electric utilities. However, the biggest barrier is psychological. The construction community is typically conservative, and is concerned about the liability they may take on with the responsibility of installing energy-generation systems. Further, prosperity has coincided with (relatively) low energy costs to create an instinctive wastefulness in first-world culture, even as environmentalism becomes a more mainstream value.

Most architects and engineers are remarkably resistant to energy and environmental issues. Few try to bridge the gap between commercial or academic design and "green" design. And yet there is an enormous opportunity waiting. Why not address the long-standing disconnect—even hostility—between modern architecture and the environment? We clad buildings with opaque skins that reject daylight and absorb heat, while inside lights burn, creating more heat that is blown outside by air-conditioning units, which are oversized to carry off the heat they produce themselves. The skin of a building should instead gather as much energy as possible and direct it to where it is most needed. It is entirely complementary to combine PV systems with daylighting and the collection of thermal energy. The end product should be a more interesting, more comfortable building.

Eventually buildings will be obligated (as a matter of responsible design practice and economic necessity, if not of building code) to use as much of the renewable energy potential as possible for a given site and program. Many buildings will produce an excess of energy, feeding it into the local grid for use by others. When this happens, these buildings will cease to be an environmental problem, and instead become part of the solution.

We believe this will be a benefit to everyone. There will be a fundamental shift in building design, from the negative to the positive. On the level of environmental quality, building design will cease to focus on negative effects—savings and mitigation and reduction—to a positive one of clean energy production, of maximization. It is our hope that a similar shift will take place on the plane of design. By facing tangible challenges of passive and active engagement with the environment, architects will have the opportunity to create new forms and reinterpret old ones.

Building-integrated PV is a technology as significant as air conditioning, the elevator, and the steel frame. Each of these technologies produced profound changes in social and economic patterns, while contributing to the evolution of architectural language. The time has come to put these theories to the test.

Sustainable Design Goes Mainstream

Harry Gordon, FAIA, Senior Vice President, COO

Burt Hill Kosar Rittelmann Associates
1056 Thomas Jefferson Street NW
Washington, DC 20007
www.burthill.com

After decades of intense effort by designers, architects, individuals, and organizations, a tectonic shift in design thinking has occurred: sustainability is now becoming mainstream. Some might even say it has become a societal design norm.

The advent of the LEED 2.0 system—the U.S. Green Building Council's Leadership in Energy and Environmental Design Green Building Rating System—is perhaps the most significant sign that this shift has taken place. The LEED standards, issued in Spring 2000, are creating a common understanding of what it means to build green.

Another sign of this change is that today's sustainable building and interior design products are as attractive as their non-sustainable counterparts. Moreover, they do not necessarily add costs to projects. Going green can, in fact, save money, particularly when costs are calculated over the life cycle of the building. Here are some of the most important ways that sustainable design thinking is going mainstream.

Urban Reuse

Renovating abandoned or underused structures could be considered the ultimate form of recycling. Urban reuse results in far less construction waste than demolition, is usually completed more quickly than new construction, and reduces the need for energy-consuming transportation during construction and beyond. It can breathe new life into communities and neighborhoods by creating housing, entertainment, and commerce where it may not have existed before, while also preserving the local character and charm that new construction cannot create.

Urban reuse has become a necessity as the economy soars and the demand for housing and office space outstrips new construction. In downtown Pittsburgh, for example, two 90-year-old office buildings are being renovated as luxury and loft-like apartments, placing residents close to work, theater, restaurants, entertainment, and public transportation. The Penn Avenue Apartments will all feature energy-efficient appliances and HVAC systems, and the remodeling has been designed to minimize construction waste and debris. Loft-style urban apartments are not simply about meeting housing needs, however. They indicate consumer demand for hip, unusual, urban housing that developers can fulfill by creative and sustainable renovations of underused buildings.

Natural Ventilation

Natural ventilation is gaining popularity as a comfortable, cost-effective way to cool buildings and improve indoor air quality. Properly designed natural ventilation systems can dramatically reduce energy consumption. The Pittsburgh Convention Center, scheduled to open in Spring 2001, has a natural ventilation system that will reduce the building's reliance on traditional air conditioning to the point where it will be possible to shut off the heating and air-conditioning systems for much of the year. The convention center's system was developed using a computer-modeling program that generates three-dimensional models that account for all of the natural and mechanical forces in the building that influence air flow. The models will be used to locate louvers in the roof of the building that will permit cool, outdoor air to "drop" into the building and displace lighter, warmer air, creating a continuous convection current that forces hot air up and out of the building. Fresh air will circulate through the building naturally, increasing the comfort of those in the building without requiring any additional energy consumption.

Natural Daylighting and Climate Control

By properly siting a building and using numerous

energy-efficient windows, indoor daylighting can be greatly increased. In cooler climates, this not only lights the interior, it also heats it by providing passive solar gains. In hotter climates, a building can be sited to minimize direct sunlight and roof eaves can shade the windows, reducing heat gain.

Meeting Community Standards

By following sustainable design practices, building owners and developers can now increase the size of their projects and their opportunities to raise funds for new construction. Arlington County, Virginia, for example, rewards building developers who achieve a Silver LEED rating with increases in their available floor area ratio (FAR), or development density. The zoning board also has the right to authorize additional square footage for a project based on its LEED rating, which can exceed the square footage granted to developers who do not meet LEED Silver standards. By doing this, the county gives environmentally responsible building owners and developers the opportunity to increase their rental or sale profits. In addition, some national funding institutions are linking grants to the condition that any buildings constructed or remodeled with the funds meet LEED standards. By directly tying sustainable design to grant money, these funders are further ingraining the concept that sustainable design is profitable and practical.

A More Integrated Approach

Traditionally, building design and construction has

been a segregated process where land planners, architects, engineers, interior designers, and contractors work in isolation from one another. Performing work related to their own disciplines, they tended not to consider the project in its entirety. This disjointed approach almost assures conflict and inefficiency. Today, there is a movement toward a more integrated approach where all parties meet at the beginning of a project to discuss goals and set priorities. This is particularly important in green projects where everything from siting the building to selecting the materials to zoning the mechanical systems impacts the building's overall success. Integrated design also helps to eliminate waste and error.

When developers, owners, designers, engineers, and contractors make sustainable choices, they gain more than satisfaction for acting responsibly. They also achieve significant gains in profitability. In addition to reduced waste and energy costs, workplace research has shown that improved daylighting and climate control increases employee productivity from six to 16 percent. Responsible resource management, comfortable living and working environments, and an enhanced bottom line all point toward sustainable design as the mandate of the future.

Human-Centered Sustainable Design

Kirsten Childs, ASID, Director of Interior Design, and Randolph R. Croxton, FAIA, Director of Architecture and Planning

Croxton Collaborative Architects
475 Fifth Avenue, 22nd Floor
New York, NY 10017

The work of Croxton Collaborative Architects is often characterized simply as "green" or "sustainable." We see our work taking place on a bigger canvas. We practice not just another type or style of architecture, but one dedicated to an original, valid, and enduring quality of excellence in architecture that serves client, community, and humankind.

There are three core qualities that inform the firm's decisions and actions.

- *Environmental:* The foundation and precursor of all design effort is a deep understanding of natural systems. The unique confluence, interaction, and history of natural systems at a site provides a powerful framework of assets and opportunities. By understanding a project's starting point in nature, we can learn how to proceed on a restorative/ regenerative path.

- *Sustainable:* The ultimate revelation of action and consequence, sustainability makes possible the informed introduction of the "built" into the "natural" world, with full understanding of the future consequences of that action. (Collectively, environmental/sustainable insights empower us to approach building as a restorative act in nature).

- *Humanistic:* There is no meaning for architecture without human-centered values. From shaping the client's mission to a deep involvement with each community and its issues to social/economic equity to ergonomic design and the minimization of toxic materials, each step of our design process is grounded in humanistic concerns.

Croxton Collaborative has transformed these values into a fully formed design methodology. Our approach has defined many of the criteria now being used to establish the goals and practices of sustainable design. Our 1987 design of the Natural Resources Defense Council (NRDC) headquarters in New York stands as a seminal project, one that proved that to be "environmental," one must address the full ecology of a building: light, air, energy, and human health and well-being. This single project established that a sustainable approach to the built environment enhances quality of life, adds value, reduces environmental degradation, and is achievable within market-rate costs.

Today, an intensively studied body of work confirms the "value-added" qualities of high-performance buildings. Books such as Joseph J. Romm's *Cool Companies* and the Rocky Mountain Institute's *Greening the Bottom Line* examine the massive savings to be realized in terms of energy conservation and productivity, not to mention human comfort and safety, to be realized from this more considered design approach. Often, when sustainable strategies are embraced, there is a heavy emphasis on energy and resource conservation—factors easily quantifiable in terms of economic benefit. However, there is a growing consensus that the human-centered aspects of sustainable design—issues of health, well-being, comfort, and safety—offer even greater economic returns.

How can these disparate goals—human well-being and the enhancement of the environment—be addressed by one set of functional and aesthetic objectives? In an environmental/sustainable design philosophy, it's a truism that critical factors that optimize building performance and reduce environmental impact also enhance human well-being. These factors include thermal comfort, access to daylight, the time of day, and the season of the year (a dynamic and invigorating "echo" of nature), blended artificial/natural light, anti-glare lighting, high-quality indoor air with low or no toxicity sources, and strategies to avoid the growth of microbial/fungal contamination. Flexible, ergonomic furniture and personal control over a worker's immediate environs—light, air, temperature, acoustics—empower people in the workplace.

Thermal comfort is achieved through climate-specific studies of the building's glazing, shell, systems, and materials and their dynamic interaction with minimized heating, ventilating and air-conditioning systems (HVAC). Energy and air-movement simulation models are used to make these interactions visible and quantifiable. The "inputs" to these models and the skilled interpretation of data are central to achieving optimum results.

The beneficial effects of daylight on human beings have long been recognized. Individuals isolated from natural light become disoriented and listless, and workplaces absent daylight are less productive. Access to natural light, even "borrowed" light, also provides a sense of time of day and season of the year that resonates in the human subconscious, reinforcing circadian rhythms and supporting well-being.

Newer types of glass treatments utilized in environmental/sustainable projects allow for high levels of natural light while reducing solar gain. High R-values associated with orientation-specific "smart" glazing ensure a more even distribution of heating and cooling, creating a building with reduced vulnerability to the traverse of the sun and greater occupant comfort.

Enhancement of the thermal shell and access to daylight contribute to energy conservation, as does a blended natural and artificial (electric) lighting system. Many systems and lamps available today are responsive to photocell technology (for daylight dimming) and occupancy sensors. These controls can contribute as much as 35 percent to the efficiency of a lighting system. Combined with electronic or solid state ballasts and high-efficiency lamps, savings can amount to 80 percent over traditional systems.

Indoor air quality is central to a healthy, safe workplace. There are two main sources of pollution in a building. The first is the HVAC system, where microbial and fungal contamination can occur in the damp, humid conditions or as a result of standing water in or near the system intake. This type of biocontamination can cause a condition known as "building related illness." Familiar examples of microbial contamination include Legionnaire's Disease; *Stachybotrys Atra*, a highly toxic fungus that can produce mycotoxins; and *Cladosporium*, which can live in ductwork and under raised floor systems. Heavy filtration at the air-intake and mixing equipment can reduce the level of contaminants.

The second group of contaminant sources is pollution introduced through building materials, finishes, and products, often called "loads." These multiple sources of contamination can cause a phenomenon known as "sick building syndrome," where occupants suffer from a general malaise and respiratory discomfort, headache, allergies, and eye irritation.

Specific illness and/or causative agents cannot be easily identified.

Construction and fit-up materials and the chemicals used to enhance their performance can be extremely deleterious to human health. This has made us aware of the importance of research into the characteristics of materials: how they are grown, gathered, quarried, or mined; whether or not they are finite, renewable, or naturally sustainable; their processing, levels of toxicity, and health effects; their maintainability, durability, and options for final disposal. Concerns about health and productivity are thus tightly inter-woven with resource conservation. While much can be done with increased ventilation, high filtration levels, and multiple air changes per hour, the real resolution to minimizing toxic loads is in limiting their presence in the first place. This requires rigorous research at the outset to minimize or eliminate any products or materials known to affect human health.

Providing some level of personal control over one's immediate environs enhances well-being and productivity. It is possible to allow workers to open a window, fine-tune the level of cooling or heat in their office or area, and decrease sound by deploying sound-absorbent panels. These "enablers" go to the heart of green design. They drive the work of our office, and they are the reason that our projects are exemplars of sustainable design.

Less formal and more open workspaces are also an important strategy in environmental/sustainable and human-centered projects. Flexible furniture, easily adjusted and ergonomically conforming to the human dimension, is essential to avoid discomfort and repetitive stress injuries such as carpal tunnel syndrome.

Rather than "green" or "sustainable," our perspective might best be called "high performance design," as it encompasses a fresh approach to planning, architecture, and interior design. It is a philosophy, a methodology, and a blending of art and science that goes beyond the designing and construction of buildings. This unique level of performance is achieved through close coordination among team members and disciplines, customized simulation tools, an advanced understanding of air quality, materials conservation, and waste stream management. All of these tactics are used in pursuit of the ultimate goal—to create buildings that "give back" to the environment, sustain and restore natural habitat and human health, and contribute to quality of life.

Traditional design excellence, the "art" in the art and science of architecture, remains at the center of our practice. But the bedrock qualities of environmental/sustainable and human-centered design—so old and yet so new—are the soul of the process, allowing us to reassert the deeper values and meanings to be found in the built environment.

The Eco-Office: Tomorrow's Workplace, Today

Robert Watson, Senior Analyst, and
Adam Cox, Senior Analyst

Natural Resources Defense Council
40 West 20th Street
New York, NY 10011
www.nrdc.org

In June 1996, the Natural Resources Defense Council (NRDC), a 30-year-old national environmental organization, moved into a new 20,000-square-foot space in Washington, D.C., that is one of the most environmentally friendly offices in the United States.

This eco-office is located at 1200 New York Avenue, in a new 12-story gray granite building constructed for the American Association for the Advancement of Science (AAAS). The building was designed by Henry Cobb, of the renowned architectural firm of

Pei, Cobb, Freed, and Partners. New York architects Croxton Collaborative was responsible for the building's energy-efficiency and environmental features. The AAAS building boasts an air-conditioning system that does not rely on ozone-depleting CFCs or HCFCs, formaldehyde-free carpets and ceiling tiles, and innovative architectural daylighting features that help cut energy consumption by 50 percent. These environmental aspects of the AAAS building were a primary impetus for NRDC to locate there.

The Washington office represents the culmination of a 10-year greening process of all four of the organization's offices nationwide. All of NRDC's offices now demonstrate innovative energy and environmental design and provide valuable examples of what's currently possible in the field of office construction. This newest addition also shows how much has changed since our greening effort began in 1987, when we began working with Croxton Collaborative on our New York offices. Over 90 percent of the environmental materials used in the Washington office were not available when we started designing our New York headquarters.

Costs

NRDC incurred additional first costs of $9.50 per square foot for the build-out of its space. About $2 of this was a result of additional design costs, and about $2.90 was attributable to environmental and energy efficiency features. The rest was for items such as an internal stairwell, additional security requirements, etc. All of these extra costs are a part of moving up the learning curve of environmental building and the early stage in which some of these materials and practices find themselves. As these products mature, it is our belief that costs will decline, making many green products competitive with standard materials.

Some of the extra costs of environmental design will be easily paid back through reduced operating costs and expected increases in productivity, including reduced absenteeism. In our New York office, for example, NRDC staff have shown high satisfaction with the ability to control their lighting as well as the ability to have visual access to daylight in the corridors through clerestories and other architectural devices.

Design Principles

NRDC established the following set of environ-mental design principles that guided our design and product choices.

- Demonstrate environmental leadership in a state-of-the-art eco-sensitive and energy-efficient office that can be a learning tool and an inspirational example.

- Use innovative, natural, renewable, low-toxic and/or recycled materials.

- Protect and enhance indoor air quality.

- Demonstrate reductions in wood use and showcase products made from wood harvested from independently certified, well-managed forests.

- Demonstrate cutting-edge, cost-effective energy-efficient lighting design, appliances, and computer equipment.

Environmental Materials

NRDC installed two different wall systems that have environmental benefits: solid compressed straw panels and synthetic gypsum wallboard sandwiching steel studs. In the United States, straw is currently disposed of by open-air burning, which causes severe seasonal air-quality problems over large regions of the country. Using straw-based materials reduces the amount of material burned and thus reduces pollutants. NRDC also used a compressed straw core for its doors instead of particleboard, reducing wood use. The synthetic gypsum wallboard employs an industrial by-product from power plant desulfurization or titanium dioxide manufacturing that would need to be disposed of otherwise. Using a synthetic equivalent also reduces the amount of gypsum that is mined, avoiding the financial and environmental costs of that process.

The paints used had very low volatile organic compound (VOC) levels, from 80 to 99 percent lower than conventional paints. VOCs contribute to indoor air-quality problems as well as to outdoor ozone pollution. In addition, all of the adhesives used have reduced VOC levels, and some do not contain any reportable hazardous material content at all.

For carpeting we used a solution-dyed nylon carpet that will be recycled at the end of its life. Carpet recycling programs are growing rapidly and will reduce the use of fossil fuels as well as reduce landfill waste. Other flooring materials included true linoleum, which is made from all natural ingredients, rather than vinyl tile. Vinyl is made using chlorine compounds that have been implicated as endocrine disrupters. The ceramic tile we installed contains 70 percent recycled glass from windshields and plate glass. This tile requires less energy to produce and keeps extra waste out of the landfill. Mineral fiber-free ceiling tile was installed to respond to concerns about microfibers getting into the office air through the ventilation system.

NRDC demonstrated several environmental products for use as shelving and countertop substrate (the material underneath the finish or laminate) as substitutes or replacements for wood-based products containing toxic resins, such as plywood or particleboard. These products are made from agricultural waste, straw, or recycled junk mail instead of wood, reducing pressure on our nation's forests.

We also wanted to showcase products made of responsibly harvested wood. Certified well-managed forests maintain natural forest structures that are the antithesis of "cut-and-run" logging practices, reducing ecosystem degradation, biodiversity loss, air and water pollution, destruction of natural scenery, and economic instability.

Several pieces of custom furniture were commissioned. Fabrics used for their cushions were created from a completely retooled manufacturing process that uses no toxic materials and produces no waste. Most of the countertops throughout the office are finished with a material that looks something like marble and feels like plastic, but is made up of recycled newsprint, soybean flour, coloring, and adhesives.

Energy Efficiency Measures

Efficient lighting systems, computers, and appliances save about 60 percent of the energy consumed in a conventional office space. Daylighting combined with efficient lighting equipment and energy-conserving design use 65 percent less power than a conventional system—about 0.5 watts per square foot, compared with the average use of 1.4 watts per square foot. Computing and appliance energy was reduced by half through the use of the most energy-efficient equipment available. The energy savings from these measures results in thousands of pounds of avoided emissions of carbon dioxide, sulfur dioxide, and nitrogen oxides.

Finally, NRDC's daily operations were examined for ways to reduce environmental impacts and safeguard the health of our employees. We purchased an economical drinking water purification system and use organic, shade-grown coffee. In addition, all of our paper and most of our office supplies have significant post-consumer recycled content.

Measuring Gains

Energy costs for the Washington, D.C., office are currently included in NRDC's rent payment, so we receive no direct benefit from the energy efficiency, though it is clear that the energy measures taken are very cost-effective. Productivity gains in a dynamic office setting are more difficult to measure. However, evidence suggests that improved environmental conditions in buildings can led to productivity increases ranging from six percent to 15 percent. Annual labor costs range between $175 to $200 per square foot, compared with energy costs ranging between $1.75 and $2 per square foot. Thus, a one percent to two percent productivity improvement is roughly equivalent in economic terms to the total cost of energy. Several of the features of the D.C. office for which NRDC paid extra are thought to enhance productivity, such as the internal stairwell, though these features are not necessarily "environmental."

SECTION 2:

BUILDING COMMUNITY

Biomimicry, Biophilia, and Building Community

William D. Browning, Senior Research Associate, Green Development Services

Rocky Mountain Institute
Green Development Services
1739 Snowmass Creek Road
Snowmass, CO 81654
www.rmi.org

"What is the use of a house if you haven't got a tolerable planet to put it on?"
—*Henry David Thoreau*

The Inn of the Anasazi is a popular four-star hotel in Santa Fe, New Mexico, just off the edge of the Governor's Plaza. It has not always been so. The building began its life in 1965 as the steel-and-concrete offices of the New Mexico state prison system and a juvenile detention center for Santa Fe—not exactly the most auspicious start for a luxury hotel.

Fifteen years later, it was reopened as the Inn of the

Anasazi. The building's original skin had been completely stripped off, and the hotel was built around the old structure. The finished building resembles an outsized adobe structure, clad in dark brown stucco and with traditional New Mexican features inside, like viga-and-latilla ceilings and tile floors. It is quite beautiful, and as green buildings go, it is a pretty good one—it recycled an existing building in an urban fabric, almost all of the building materials were locally sourced, it's reasonably energy- and water-efficient, and a lot of attention was paid to indoor air quality. But still you might ask, "Okay, that's a good green building, but why should I care about this one?"

Well, this one's also about the people and the fabric of Santa Fe. Local artisans made much of the furniture. The toiletries are produced by a small community north of Santa Fe, using Native American herbs, and are marketed through the hotel. The restaurant gets 90 percent of its food from a network of local organic suppliers, predominantly land-grant Spanish families. If these families' land goes out of agricultural production, it will be taxed at full development rates, which means they would lose or be forced to sell it, probably to developers. Instead, the families grow healthy, organic food, which gives them income and an ability to stay on in an exceedingly and increasingly expensive market.

Every time we investigate another aspect of the hotel's operation, we find some new way in which it has woven itself into the social and environmental fabric of Santa Fe. The restaurant, for example, closes the food production loop by sending excess food to local homeless shelters, table scraps to compost, and kitchen scraps to an organic pig farm. The staff is made up of the three cultures of Santa Fe: Latino, Native American, and Anglo. This diverse group of people leads ethnic-dispute resolution sessions at the hotel for the City of Santa Fe. The guests never find out about any of this. It is just the way the place is run.

What are the results of all of this? There's almost no staff turnover. The Inn of the Anasazi runs at 83 percent occupancy, and 50 percent above its original financial projections. This project tells us where we are now with the reconception of real estate development. It is not necessarily limited to the standard list of issues—energy efficiency, indoor air quality, habitat protection, pedestrian-based planning, green materials specification, etc. Instead, it involves moving beyond technologies and techniques to thinking about how a project proactively weaves itself into the social and ecological fabric of a community. But we have more to learn.

"Those who look for the laws of nature as a support for their new works collaborate with the creator."
—*Antonio Gaudí*

Last week I stood in awe of a 15-foot-tall scrub oak perched on a narrow ridge 600 feet above the Columbia River. The old tree only had three branches, the lowest branch reaching 25 feet out from under the tall Douglas firs around it. This stunning cantilever is more than 12 inches in diameter at its base and carries a canopy of leaves at the other end. It stands up to winds that can reach 80 miles per hour. It is made from sugars, starches, and water. No human-made structure comes close.

There are many other extraordinary examples of the natural world's materials and systems. Spiders produce a fiber using crickets, flies, and room-temperature water that is stronger than steel at the same diameter. Coral reefs produce concrete in warm sea water. Abalone in cold sea water produce a ceramic stronger than any manmade type. Healthy ecosystems recycle wastes and produce no detrimental by-products, just clean water, oxygen, and food.

Trying to figure out how nature accomplishes such structural and systematic feats, and how we can apply them to human creations, is called biomimicry. The first attempts at biomimicry for buildings have been interesting. Eastgate, an office complex in Harare, Zimbabwe, is based on the design of tropical termite mounds. In proportion to their inhabitants, these mounds are giant skyscrapers, yet they have consistently cooler interior temperatures than the surrounding air. The termites control the temperature by opening and closing vertical ventilation shafts, introducing water to evaporate in certain areas, and flapping their wings to move air. At Eastgate, fans bring fresh air in through the atrium and blow it up to the higher floors through hollow floors. It warms as it rises, then exits through the roof. At night, fans flush colder air through the building, cooling down the hollow floors. Windows are smaller than usual and heavily shaded to avoid heat gain. Eastgate, which opened in 1996, uses less than 10 percent of the energy required by a conventional building its size. Energy savings are passed on to tenants.

Another example is the Living Machine, a biological wastewater system created by John Todd that uses a series of assembled ecosystems to cleanse water. Anaerobically treated sewage enters a greenhouse that contains a series of tanks, each of which contains various species of bacteria, algae, plants, snails, fish, and other creatures. These animals and plants break down the sewage as it passes through. The result is "waste" water that exceeds EPA drinking water standards.

"We shape our dwellings, and afterwards our dwellings shape our lives."
                                              —*Winston Churchill*

Why do some places just feel right? Why are some buildings and neighborhoods vibrant with community life while others languish? Why do we perform better in some spaces than others? Some emerging answers to these questions center around our deep attachment to natural forms and nature in general, an idea called "biophilia." Harvard biologist E. O. Wilson was one of the originators of the idea; his work draws on studies of comfort and physiological responses, human evolutionary biology, and environmental psychology.

The best scientific evidence indicates that humans evolved on the savannas of Africa. It is this environment that we try to reproduce around the world: the annual burning of oak savanna by Ojibway peoples in the American Midwest, the suburban front lawn, the Japanese garden, the Moorish paradise. Analysis of the physical and psychological conditions of these environments is just beginning to be applied to buildings. An experiment at Herman Miller's SQA plant, an office furniture factory building in Zeeland, Michigan, used biophilia protocols as predictors of response to the new facility. Areas of the building that fell within the conditions of the protocol had measurable gains in worker productivity; those that were outside of the protocol did not. Positive changes in such measures as production rates, academic performance, and sales per square foot indicate improvements in the overall health and well-being of the occupants of the places that we design and build. Biophilia may give us a better way to understand how to create fundamentally better places.

If we can begin to shift our conceptions of the purpose and process of development to one that heals human and natural communities, uses nature as a mentor, and addresses occupants' physiological and psychological needs, then we will be on our way to integrating ecology and real estate. We will also have begun to answer Henry David Thoreau's plaintive question.

The Mystic View Task Force

Anne Tate,
Associate Professor, Rhode Island School of Design,
Principal, Abacus Architects & Planners

Daniel DeLisi, Planner,
Vanasse & Daylor

Abacus Architects & Planners
140 Sycamore Street
Somerville, MA 02145

Vanasse & Daylor
12730 New Brittany Boulevard, Suite 600
Ft. Myers, FL 33907
www.vanday.com

On August 25, 1999, more than 200 citizens of Somerville, Massachusetts, attended a public presentation of a proposal to develop an aging mall into a regional retail "power center"—a collection of big-box stores along the Mystic River. Community members spoke in unanimous protest. The comments were eloquent, informed, and to the point. Residents let their political leaders and the developers know that "big-box" retail, with its acres and acres of parking lots, was not an appropriate use of their waterfront land. One after another, they demanded that the developers consider higher-intensity development, urging that a high-quality, pedestrian-oriented, mixed-use urban neighborhood with expanded parks along the river would make more money, earn more tax revenue, and offer the city much-needed jobs and amenities. Stunned, the developers retreated.

For Somerville, this community involvement in land-use development marked a first. Somerville is a dense, working-class city with a diverse population, few public amenities, and a small commercial tax base. Residents have traditionally been excluded from development decisions and have made little effort to become involved. Public officials have welcomed whatever development they could get. The opportunities of this site, made visible and believable by an organized and talented group of volunteers, galvanized the desire for change and justice in a community too long forgotten by planners and politicians.

Not only did the residents of Somerville, organized by the Mystic View Task Force, succeed in influencing the course of development and planning in the city, they also developed an exciting model for opposing locally unwanted land uses (LULUs)—in this case big-box retail. How did it happen?

Mystic View refers to approximately 150 acres of land along the Mystic River in East Somerville, directly north of Boston's Charlestown neighborhood. To the west, an elevated portion of I-93, the most heavily traveled arterial into Boston, cuts off the site from the rest of East Somerville. The site has a long history as a place of production, warehousing, and transport. It has been the site of several ship-yards, the nation's largest food warehouse, and a Ford Motors plant, which was a major regional employer. It is Somerville's only waterfront area.

In the spring of 1998, the local state representative, Patricia Jehlen, invited Anne Tate, from the Boston Society of Architects Task Force on Growth Management, to give a slide presentation to Somerville residents on "Guiding Growth." At that meeting, concerns in the community about the pending redevelopment of the riverfront were crystallized and a task force was born. The group rechristened the site "Mystic View" to create an awareness in the community that a riverfront existed, albeit tucked behind a sea of parking lots and vacant space.

From its inception the Mystic View Task Force (MVTF), wanted to create an inclusive process to collect opinions and ideas from a large cross-section of residents. Tate had extensive experience in orga-nizing community design workshops, often called charrettes. The Mystic View Task Force decided to plan a one-day event to explore development ideas and to create their own proposals for the site.

Over the next year MVTF prepared for the charrette by organizing a series of meetings to solicit community ideas. The task force built support for the process through print, TV, and radio media presentations to elected officials, the business community, residents, and property owners.

In these discussions, several key issues emerged for the site: open space, tax income, jobs, access to the site, and, most important, expanded use of the Mystic River.

The MVTF Design Committee put together a talented group of architects and planners, many of whom live in Somerville, to design pre-charrette "idea starters." The task force believed it more useful and educational for participants to react to and work with several different design ideas. Over three meetings the design committee drafted six concepts for discussion.

On May 22, 1999, more than 150 residents gathered to voice their opinions about the future of Mystic View. MVTF organized the day into three educational presentations, each followed by small group working sessions. Participants discussed what they would like from the future of the site through the question, "If you came to a reunion on this site in the year 2025, describe what you hope the site will be like."

Task force member Wig Zamore, a real estate development consultant, placed the site in the context of the greater Boston region, making the case for its desirability. He then presented a compelling financial analysis demonstrating that higher-intensity development could bring in 10 times the number of jobs and taxes as big-box retail would provide. This analysis-made-simple empowered community residents without any design or planning background to better assess options for the site. Participants again broke into small groups to create their own designs for the Mystic View site. The visual "idea starters" proved effective in encouraging them to imagine new alternatives. Each group received a base map of the site, tracing paper, drawing utensils, and sample cut-out land uses and building types. With these tools, each group created a different proposal, all with development and open space, taking advantage of the water-front location.

On August 25th, when Taurus Investment and National Development of New England walked into the next meeting, they met a well-organized and motivated community. Their proposal shocked the 200 residents and elected officials. It offered exactly what the community had already said it did not want. They further antagonized people by calling the proposal Riverside Plaza, a change from the earlier name "Assembly Square," which alluded to the historic Ford Motors plant—a historical reference that residents had embraced. According to Pat Jehlen, the artist renderings of beautiful Home Depots, Kmarts, and giant entrance archways only served to further insult the community.

In response to the public outrage, Mayor Kelly Gay convened a summit a few weeks later that included the 15 landlords who own the site. She succeeded in negotiating an agreement to delay all development on the site until the city completed a master plan. The city then hired the Cecil Group, a Boston-based architecture and design firm, to draft a plan for the site.

By the time the Cecil Group started its process, the community had the knowledge and capacity to voice their opinions, concerns, and desires. Somerville residents' efforts had a large impact on the direction of the Cecil Group's plan. MVTF set the standard for comparing and critiquing the consultant's work. Early on, the consultant was skeptical about the viability of a transit stop on the site. At the community's insistence, the Cecil Group investigated the idea further and it quickly became the cornerstone of the plan. At every juncture residents compared the Cecil Group's proposal with the community-based designs. Would the consultant's plan deliver 30 new acres of open space, 30,000 new jobs, and $30 million in revenues?

The work of the Mystic View Task Force is distinguished from many similar struggles to fight off unwanted land uses by its overt use of design. Members spent hours networking with city and state officials, business leaders, and academic institutions. They sought out a large cross-section of stakeholders to involve in the process. Throughout, they effectively used a well designed and developed alternative vision to inspire supporters and convince opponents of their argument.

On June 22, 2000, the city's Board of Aldermen unanimously passed a resolution stating that it "supports the vision for the redevelopment of Assembly Square articulated by the Mystic View Task Force and supports the Administration in imposing conditions and design standards." The mayor dismissed a minimally revised big-box proposal, confident that she had other options that represented a better future for the city. The task force is continuing its efforts to increase public understanding of the issues, to interest development partners in the site, and to bolster the city's efforts to regulate development on the site.

In Somerville, a precedent has been set. Residents will no longer accept development scenarios that focus simply on big-box retail. Activists are now influencing development in other parts of the city as well. A community that previously expected to be a victim of other interests has now taken over the process, claiming it for themselves.

Haymount: Planning a Sustainable Town

*John A. Clark, Principal, and
David A. Tice,
The John A. Clark Company*

*Neal I. Payton, AIA
Torti Gallas & Partners • CHK*

The John A. Clark Company
7912 Railroad Street
Dunn Loring, VA 22027

Torti Gallas & Partners • CHK
1300 Spring Street, Suite 400
Silver Spring, MD 20910
www.tortigallaschk.com

Over the past several decades, planners and sociologists have detailed the human toll exacted by our culture's reliance on technological progress. Though great strides have been made in science and its application, even to the point of prolonging and enhancing human life, the increasing specialization required by a technologically based society has had the effect of fragmenting our civilization. Social solutions were attempted in the early 1960s, followed soon after by an environmental response; however, neither has proven successful on its own. To balance nature and the human spirit in one place and form, we must seek a holistic solution, a vision that embraces both an environmental and a social contract.

A new town that embodies this solution is being planned in Virginia along the Rapahannock River. This town, Haymount, will foster the healing of nature and the human spirit. Its plan and design account for natural resource protection, pollution prevention, appropriate transportation solutions, the fostering of vital community life, and the need for sustainability in design and practice.

Most typical land-use requirements promote low-density suburban sprawl, destroying natural habitat and necessitating automobile travel to fulfill every human need in the process. Haymount's 4,000 homes, 250,000 square feet of retail space, and a half-million square feet of office and commercial space will restore life-sustaining connections between the land and its occupants. The initial phase of the project, the construction of the wastewater treatment plant, should begin in early 2001; the first houses will start to be built a few months after that.

Engaging the noted architecture and town planning firm of Duany Plater-Zyberk, Haymount's master plan was aided by an intensive on-site design charrette. This process included design professionals, scientists, and local residents both in favor and opposed to the project, giving all parties a voice in the design.

Natural Resource Protection and Pollution Prevention

Before Haymount's first street was planned, consultants evaluated endangered and threatened species that were present or potentially present. Three hundred such species were identified and, in keeping with the holistic approach of the development, all their life requirements were considered, including breeding cover, foraging and perching habitat, escape cover, food sources (and their respective habitat requirements), and water.

The design of Haymount not only protects these species, it will, in some cases, actually increase habitat suitability. Existing trees were inventoried and mapped, with an analysis of how their growth would affect homes and wildlife in the future. The information was incorporated into site development plans to protect as many specimen trees as possible. And 50,000 new native trees and shrubs will be planted, improving and increasing habitat for most species and providing shelter for migrating songbirds. Additional measures to improve habitat suitability include protection of key wildlife corridors, wetlands, and other sites; the design of green spaces as connections between habitats; planting specifications that establish extensive canopies of native species chosen for their utility to wildlife; stormwater-management designs to create additional wetland habitats; water-quality protection measures, including controls over fertilizers and pesticides; and an environmental education area and program to build a strong community commitment to conservation and habitat improvement.

The regulation of public and private plantings is crucial to the making of place, the nurturing of wildlife, and the preservation of environmental integrity. Thus, Haymount's form is governed by a landscape code that encompasses a tree program that requires the use of mostly native species of trees and shrubs for landscaping, reducing the need for watering as well as fertilizer and pesticide application. A program of organic and natural predators will be implemented as part of an integrated pest-management program.

Haymount's stormwater-control measures employ vegetation as primary and/or secondary structural elements to manage runoff, secure soil, and protect water quality. These techniques capture and treat non-point-source pollutants, allowing natural aquifer recharge and eliminating ground- or surface-water impairment. The full range of water-management practices employed include constructed wetlands, porous pavement, fascines, grass-and-block parking areas, grassed swales, and biotechnical slope protection—measures proven effective not only for erosion control, but also for nutrient reduction, soil infiltration, stream or river restoration, and wetland creation.

Combining sequence batch technology, advanced tertiary treatment, and constructed wetlands, the town's state-of-the-art wastewater-treatment system will discharge water cleaner than what it draws from the river. Ecological considerations also govern the delivery of Haymount's drinking water. The intake system consists of a shallow vertical well with a series of horizontal fingers that extend under the riverbed. This advanced system avoids disturbing the aquifer, the river bottom, or the riverbank, thereby preserving groundwater, aquatic vegetation, and fish.

Recognizing that wildlife, atmospheric conditions, and hydrologic influences do not follow property boundaries, Haymount's environmental program is without borders. Before ground was broken at Haymount, the environmental management team secured over 1,000 acres of conservation easements, successfully designated several historic districts, and assisted in the development of numerous land-stewardship plans.

Transportation

Haymount's transportation system assures environmental, economic, and social sustainability through a design that relieves congestion and programs aimed at reducing vehicle miles traveled per household and vehicle household trips. These goals will be met by establishing a pedestrian- and bicycle-friendly environment supplemented by a timed-transfer shuttle bus system; a mixed-use pattern of land development that includes major employment opportunities; reduced commercial parking requirements; and programs to encourage employers to institute programs that manage transportation demand.

The creation of a pedestrian-friendly environment is critical to Haymount's success. The town plan centers on the idea of the "five minute walk"—most residents' needs (buying a gallon of milk, for example) should be easily and quickly accessible without using a car. No residence is greater than a quarter mile from a town or village center and a shuttle bus stop. This allows residents the choice of walking for some of their trips. It also reduces miles traveled by car and, more important, "cold starts," the greatest component of auto pollution.

The town plan also mitigates traffic congestion, which limits air pollution still further by reducing idling time. Road width is reduced by adopting a configuration typical of prewar American towns and villages, slowing traffic and encouraging the use of public streets as public spaces. These narrower streets feel better to the pedestrian because of their greater degree of spatial enclosure. The introduction of alleys reduces the need for curb cuts, minimizing opportunities for automobiles to cross sidewalks while enhancing on-street parking opportunities. All of these characteristics help to reduce vehicle speed, enhance pedestrian comfort, and, coincidentally, improve auto safety.

The resident whose transportation needs extend beyond a quarter-mile will have access to a shuttle bus system connecting to the Virginia Railway Express commuter line into Washington, D.C. The bus system will also provide regular intra-community transport for the elderly, the young, and those who choose not to own an automobile. Located in village centers adjacent to convenience stores, as well as at employment centers, schools, and civic institutions, bus stops will be part of an extensive program of "civic art" to be places where one may actually enjoy the wait.

Transportation issues cannot be addressed solely by mass transit, which will capture about half of the car trips for work-related travel. A serious effort to provide jobs in Haymount is the most important aspect of traffic capture. An economic development plan with a goal of creating 1.2 jobs per household is being implemented. Fiber-optic lines will be installed, connecting to buildings designed to be twenty-first-century workplaces. An active recruitment effort of companies is being undertaken to meet these employment goals.

A Vital Community Life

The postwar suburb is a model of social and economic segregation. Zoning laws are the primary culprit—they mandate large-lot subdivisions and separate low-income "pod" developments while prohibiting accessory housing (such as apartments above stores or garages) and mixing land uses and lot sizes in one area. By physically segregating uses, these ordinances increase land and development costs while virtually mandating the use of an automobile for every errand. Moreover, such enforced homogeneity of building types cannot respond to changes in one's own family, such as children growing up and parents growing old.

Haymount addresses these fundamental shortcomings through its housing and land-use mix, its pedestrian-friendly environment, and its provision for a range of civic institutions and amenities that nurture community life. Affordable housing is to be constructed in every section of the development, and it will be available in a range of forms, recognizing the diverse constituency for such housing: elderly residents, young people, single parents, and couples and families of limited income.

A town that encourages walking not only requires less intensive use of the automobile, it also fosters a sense of community by providing for the establishment of relationships through encounters on the sidewalk. It also enhances security by keeping eyes on the street. Haymount's rules that govern the siting of private buildings help shape the space of public and commercial life. Generally, they prescribe building use, placement, height, permitted encroachments (such as front porches, which are encouraged), and the location of parking for each of the eight different lot types and sizes. Other codes, which regulate construction materials and techniques, are intended to enhance urban coherence, pedestrian friendliness and "sense of place."

The spirit of community must be nurtured to form a web of connectedness between people and place. Religious institutions have been asked to locate in Haymount, on sites selected for their prominence. Parks also play a role in forming bonds of community, and they will be designed and constructed with funds provided by the developer to accommodate a range of public uses, including sports, leisure, and public congregation. River frontage will either be constructed into park space or protected in its natural form; none will be privatized.

Sustainability

Perhaps the most far-reaching environmental component of Haymount is its sustainability program. Using sophisticated ecological and economic modeling techniques developed by the management team, the flow of resources and transactions among all the major economic sectors and the commodity groups will be evaluated. This will include not only direct effects—for example, the impact of healthy building materials—but indirect ones as well, such as household expenditures. With the size of Haymount's economic contribution as powerful leverage, the team will work with suppliers and other businesses to effect environmentally responsible voluntary agreements and identify funding sources to assist businesses in the region to meet strict environmental standards.

Putting the Emerald Back in the Emerald City

Nathaniel Cormier, Associate

Jones & Jones Architects and Landscape Architects
105 South Main Street
Seattle, WA 98104
www.jonesandjones.com

Seattle, a city of hills overlooking Elliott Bay, sits in the Puget Sound Trough, between Washington's Cascade and Olympic mountain ranges. Early European explorers of the region beheld foothills and river valleys shadowed by dense woods of thousand-year-old Western red cedar and Douglas fir. These visitors witnessed timeless exchanges between the temperate rain forest and the sea. The sea brought the climate and weather necessary for the trees to reach their awesome size, while the forest in turn nourished the sea with minerals, nutrients, water, and wildlife. The cyclical migrations of the salmon are a powerful symbol of this interdependence.

Mid-nineteenth-century American settlers met native peoples whose food came mostly from the rivers, bays, and ocean and whose homes, canoes, tools, and even clothes came from the cedars. These native peoples had flourished here "since the Raven released the sun" by recognizing sacred duties to the land in exchange for its gifts. Though we cannot return Seattle to this primordial state, we can learn to listen to the land—the rain still falls, the sun still visits, a few salmon still leap—and restore the qualities of this place that will sustain and nourish us.

A Forest Banished

Settlers felled the giant trees with abandon to clear land for farming and to carve a settlement from the seemingly endless forest. San Francisco was rebuilt after the Great Fire with Seattle timber. Turn-of-the-century Seattle boomed as the jumping-off point for the Klondike Gold Rush and soon a major port and industrial city was born. Eventually, the great rivers were straightened, the streams buried, the hills sluiced, the mud flats filled, and nearly all the original vegetation stripped from the land.

Today the pressure of a runaway tech economy and an influx of new residents are straining Seattle. Open space, other than parking lots, is hard to come by in a city booming with new office and residential development, and the forests of the surrounding region are being consumed by suburban sprawl. An analysis of satellite photography by American Forests, America's oldest conservation group, shows that while 10 percent of Seattle was heavily treed in 1972, over half of that vegetation was lost by 1996. The very identity of Seattle, the Emerald City, is at stake as we allow its trees to fall and pavement to run rampant.

Desperately Seeking Salmon

The 1999 listing of Puget Sound Chinook and eight other Northwest salmon species under the Endangered Species Act, as well as dramatic declines in Orca whale (up the food chain) and herring (down the food chain) populations, indicate that the entire Puget Sound ecosystem is imperiled. There are numerous Federal regulations aimed at restoring water quality and salmon habitat, but regulatory solutions only address isolated problems. We need a holistic approach to free us from an endless string of narrowly defined problems and solutions.

Replacing underutilized impervious surfaces with forest greatly slows and reduces stormwater runoff and recharges the aquifer, providing a low-cost, natural approach to maintaining clean water and protecting Elliott Bay and its salmon. Land near waterways is particularly important because riparian forest plays a crucial role in regulating water flows, protecting water quality, preventing stream bank erosion, and providing food and shade for fish and wildlife.

More Than Potted Plants

The full potential value of forested places to the community must be included in future planning and development in the city. Forests create healthy terrestrial systems for people and wildlife. They maintain comfortable temperatures, clean pollutants from the air, and produce oxygen. Bringing back the forest would make Seattle an even more wonderful place to live while saving us billions of dollars in stormwater infrastructure, health, and energy costs.

A healthy urban forest is more than a streetscape of large potted plants. Its integrity is a function of its vertical and horizontal structure—the roots, microbes, soil, ground topography, ground cover, shrubbery, understory, and canopy; the patches and corridors harboring wildlife and connecting important natural features; and its species and age diversity—a range of native species appropriate to a variety of microclimates; seedlings, mature vegetation, even fallen "nurse logs." Also key are its relationship to built structures and systems—proximity to neighborhoods, dimensions of streetscapes; its roles as transportation greenway and stormwater blueway; its self-regulation—independence from intensive regimes of mowing, pruning, irrigating, fertilizing, and chemical spraying; and the engagement and stewardship of its people—the coordinated roles of local and regional agencies, schools, NGOs, and businesses.

Think It and Sing It Into Being

Human ingenuity gives us the power to craft complex and enriching places that simultaneously address environmental, economic, and social issues on many levels. Consider Seattle from the perspective of "biourbanism"—urban design that mimics biological processes. Our city can become a rich community of life, energy, and material cycling through a network of sustaining places. When we marry the principles of landscape ecology to the best precedents of urbanism, we will find that places that are great for salmon are also great for people. In fact, Sustainable Seattle found in a recent poll that many Seattle citizens recognize the health of wild salmon runs to be a significant indicator of the overall environmental health of watersheds and quality of life in the region.

We can develop rich and enduring concepts that reconnect us to the Puget Sound bioregion while addressing fundamental needs. Opportunities to bring back our forest lurk in every median strip, right-of-way, street end, hill slope, backyard, rooftop, and parking lot. What if every street had a tree-lined creek that would divert stormwater and clean out roadway pollutants and car exhaust? What if every schoolyard had a bosque of trees to filter out air pollution and provide a shady place for playing tag? What if every block had a park with a pond to retain the neighborhood's stormwater and double as a swimming hole? What if all our waterfront parks included wooded streams inviting to salmon? What if all these interventions were coordinated with protecting and enhancing existing natural areas for greater habitat connectivity and recreational opportunities? In the end, Seattle would become a diverse forest habitat that would give back to us for eons.

Nature into Cities and Cities into the Human Heart

No community, whether city or forest, stands still. Each has dynamic elements of stone, wood, flesh, and exuberant energy animated by ancient forces of nature and history. Learning to respect these vital forces, to bring nature into cities and cities into the human heart, is fundamental to making cities not simply livable, but desirable. We can satisfy our instinct to connect with nature without chasing it beyond the edge of the city. Forests are an enduring aspect of Seattle's natural and cultural identity. Let's put the emerald back in the Emerald City.

Green Towns

Emilio Ambasz, Principal

Emilio Ambasz & Associates, Inc.
8 East 62nd Street
New York, NY 10021
www.ambasz.com

There is a great tradition in urban planning, dating back to the nineteenth century, of creating "garden cities"—semi-utopian new towns that combine the best aspects of the city and the country. The most outstanding among many enlightened practitioners of this tradition was the English architect and planner Ebenezer Howard. The garden cities he proposed at the turn of the twentieth century became the models for several suburban communities around London. His ideas were also introduced in the United States, where a number of garden cities, such as Radburn, New Jersey, were built. These American communities differed from the British models, reflecting the availability of land as well as the beginning of an automobile-determined society. In essence, they were the forerunners of what we now know as the American suburb.

Recently there has been a growing inquiry into the new American phenomena known as "edge cities"—quasi-suburban communities that have sprung up, seemingly fully grown, on the edge of larger cities. These new cities are fully empowered politically and are capable of contesting the supremacy of the older city or cities nearby. Both traditional suburbs and edge cities are attempts at finding urban solutions that will be spiritually as well as economically fulfilling. However, none of the models built so far have truly succeeded. Moreover, we have great evidence that the new cities and capitals created during this century, such as Brasilia and Ahmedabad, have been resounding failures. It is only man's infinite capacity for adaptation that lets them limpingly survive.

Therefore, we need to develop new models. Today, with the advent of modern telecommunications, personal computers, and the Internet, it is possible for a very large number of workers to perform their tasks from home, or from satellite offices. By the same token, it is no longer necessary for a company to establish headquarters in a large city in order to draw from its pool of talent, since the pool of talent can now be reached nationwide. This has already proven to be true in industries such as insurance and banking; even universities can be dispersed, broadcasting lectures and correcting students' papers over the Internet.

Of course, we do not want to foster the idea that any social group can prosper without direct physical contact. But it is true that physical contact can be designed to happen when and where it's needed, not simply the result of casual proximity. We can imagine someone working four days a week from home or from a satellite office in her small hometown, traveling to headquarters just one day a week for special meetings.

Japan has the potential to lead the way in creating new towns that can harness these possibilities. The export-oriented Japanese economy needs to develop a complementary, inner-oriented component that can satisfy the needs and longing of its citizens. Current government initiatives for investment in the country's infrastructure present an opportunity to put into practice richer and more satisfying approaches than just building highways. This is not only because of the evils inherent in building a city around the car, but also because there is no longer a need to create cities of more than 500,000 inhabitants in order to create a center capable of self-sustaining economical production. Moreover, the importance of the agricultural economy in Japan is decreasing, and the country is experiencing large migrations to medium- and large-size cities and the depopulation of rural areas. We have already seen what can happen in extreme cases of urban migration, such as, for example, in Mexico, where the big city is understood to be one of the few options for the rural poor. No society or city can thrive under the pressure of such huge numbers of migrants.

We do not want to repeat the mistakes of the old suburban models. What we are proposing instead is a new kind of town, a Green Town. We want to go beyond the suburban "house in the garden" to have the house and the garden. Some countries have already enacted enlightened legislation aimed at having the "green surround the gray"—that is, gardens surrounding buildings. What is proposed here is the green over the gray. We have spent our professional lives proposing and creating buildings that give back to the community as much green as possible. In some cases we have been able to give back 100 percent of the land in the form of gardens that occupy the same area as the ground the building covers; an example of this is our design for the Fukuoka Prefectural International Hall in Japan. This is a very simple but profound way of creating new urban structures and settlements that do not alienate the citizens from the vegetable kingdom, but rather create an architecture that is inextricably woven into greenery, into nature.

In general, European towns developed around a prince's palace or a cathedral, and its later cities grew from such an organization. By contrast, most towns built during the past century in Japan developed around the train station.

Any new Green Town created in Japan should expand on this and be created around the train station. Furthermore, the train station should go beyond its present service as the commercial center of the city to become the town hall of the city. It should concentrate in its surroundings all types of public services, from the commercial to the cultural. One example of such a train station can be seen in our design for an as yet unbuilt new town in Chiba Prefecture; in this case, the train station is turned into a vertical green garden.

The challenge here was to integrate a train station into a commercial and cultural center that feels complete and welcoming. The unique multitiered vertical garden we designed gives a sense of welcoming arrival and enclosure, establishing visual definitions of the city center, yet screens the surrounding area. It also establishes a uniform concept for new facades for the town center, which will need a clear identity from the very beginning. This new facade is composed of an open, ivy-covered structural grid containing a potted plant in each module, which would create a natural, transparent transition between the station and the surrounding town.

Similarly, our plan for the Fukuoka Prefectural International Hall building creates an innovative and powerful synergy of landscape and urban forms. A garden is created through a series of terraces that climb the full height of the building, culminating at a magnificent belvedere that offers views of the city. Within this structure, garden and building conjoin: the building returns to the city the very land it takes away by doubling the size of the existing public space while giving the city of Fukuoka a powerful and symbolic center.

Another example that might be followed is the Worldbridge Trade and Investment Center, which we designed for Baltimore, Maryland. This nine-story, 50,000-square-foot office building came about because the neighboring community would not allow any construction that could detrimentally affect their view of the countryside. The building is composed of gradually stacked, organically shaped floor plates. In the office complex, gardens are cultivated where one plate or balcony extends beyond the next. The building also has a central atrium containing a winter garden. Thus, the building has gardens for all seasons, and when it is seen from a distance it resembles a green garden.

The real estate advantages of such an office building come from the fact that every office has a view, either to the outside landscape or to the inside winter garden. More important, it does not impose harsh surfaces upon the community but rather gives it shade, light, and the changing configurations of a living garden that covers, like the skin on a peach, a very pragmatic building. One can easily imagine variations of this building utilized not only for office buildings, but also for residential apartment buildings, where the apartments would have views to the outside landscape as well as to the inner courtyards, where both children and adults could enjoy a year-round garden.

Not far from the train station of our imagined new Green Town might be a museum based on our design for the Phoenix Museum of History, in Arizona. This building is part of an ambitious revitalization program for downtown Phoenix. Nestled within a sloping earth-covered ramp and beneath a new public park, the museum gives back to the city virtually all the land that would have been taken by a traditional building. Rising to a height of 15 meters (50 feet), the earth-covered ramp in front of the museum shields existing construction from view, while still allowing unobstructed views of the park. Three sides of the Phoenix building are visible to passersby, who can see the greenery growing on top of the inclined planed roof, while the fourth side becomes a shopping street, thus maintaining a human connection with the pedestrian while increasing security on the street.

In all of these buildings and plans lies a philosophic question: What is nature and what is man-made nature? In a situation where a tree exists either because someone planted it or because someone decided to leave it there, it is imperative that we create a new definition of what we mean by man-made nature. Such a definition would have to incorporate and expand on not only the creation of gardens and public spaces, but also the creation of architecture that must be seen as just one specialized aspect of the making of man-made nature.

The Green Town presents a magnificent opportunity for a country such as Japan to give its unique answer to the problem of a society's urbanization as it passes from an industrial economy to one concerned with the creation and utilization of information. These towns can also serve as an example of the country's progressive outlook, a reflection of its deep-seated respect for nature, and, eventually, a new model for urban settlements. These Green Towns could become a wonder of the world, and a paradise.

Sydney 2000:
The Olympic Village

Neil Ingham, Principal, and
David Winley, Senior Planner

Ingham Planning
303 Pacific Highway, Suite 19
Lindfield, NSW 2070
Australia
www.newingtonvillage.com.au
www.oca.nsw.gov.au

The 2000 Olympic and Paralympic Games will take place at a number of venues throughout Sydney, Australia. The largest venue, and the focus of the most concentrated array of environmental initiatives, is Homebush Bay, a 760-hectare (1,878-acre) site in the geographic and demographic heart of the metropolitan area.

Homebush Bay has a varied and somewhat checkered past. The land once contained an armaments depot, a brickworks, and an abattoir, and for almost 50 years served as a disposal site for domestic and industrial waste. The area contains a regionally significant remnant eucalyptus forest, Aboriginal and European historic sites, and Sydney's largest remaining mangrove forests. It is also an important wetland for migratory birds from China and elsewhere in the northern hemisphere.

From these inauspicious beginnings, Homebush Bay is now being transformed into a great community asset, with many of its environmental values protected and restored by adopting Ecologically Sustainable Development (ESD) principles in a number of key areas. Sydney's bid for the 2000 Summer Olympic Games was the first to be accompanied by environmental guidelines. As a result, all work on Olympic projects has included a commitment to ESD principles. The Olympic Co-ordination Authority, established to provide facilities for the Games and manage the redevelopment of Homebush Bay, has been committed to ensuring that new development complies with the environmental promises outlined in the city's Olympic bid.

One development within Homebush Bay that embodies the principles of sustainable architecture and design is the Athlete's Village, also known as Newington Village. The Village provides a model for future urban development, integrating environmental, design, community planning, public open space, and conservation initiatives.

In August 1995, the New South Wales government invited private sector expressions of interest for designing, financing, building, and marketing Newington Village. Proponents were told the Village must incorporate high-quality urban design and innovative approaches to ESD. In 1996, the Mirvac/Lend Lease Village Consortium was announced as the winner. Newington Village is nearing completion on 84 hectares (207 acres) that had been part of the Federal armaments depot, a few minutes' walk from the main Olympic venues at Homebush Bay. The Village will contain 650 permanent dwellings, with temporary additions and 500 specially designed modular homes. During the Olympics, some 15,000 athletes and team officials from around the world will be accommodated here.

After the Games, the modular homes will be removed and additional permanent homes built. The Village will become part of the new suburb of Newington, which will have more than 2,000 dwellings, housing an estimated 5,400 people, and a high-tech business park with some 1,600 jobs.

The Village was planned on the dual principles of sustainable development and integrated design. These principles were translated into a series of clear objectives that formed the basis of the Village's planning and design. These included:

- Minimal energy use

- Minimal water use

- Minimal waste

- Maximizing human health

- Promoting biodiversity

- Maintaining cultural significance

- Creation of a vibrant community

- Creation of a commercially viable development

In order for Newington Village to become a model for future development, this last objective was particularly important.

The Village is a medium-density low-rise (two- to four-story) community that incorporates schools, shops, and community facilities. Pedestrian, bicycle, and public transportation routes have all been planned to allow access to these facilities and the adjacent Millennium Park, the newest and largest urban park in Sydney.

Newington will also become the world's largest solar-powered suburb; all the permanent houses built by the opening of the Games will include roof-top solar cells. With these cells, the Village has the potential to generate more than one million kilowatt hours of electricity per year. This "green power" will be fed into the regional electrical grid for purchase by Newington residents as well as the broader community.

A driving principle of the Village's design has been the orientation of houses to achieve the best use of solar energy. Most roads run north–south, enabling the majority of houses to have their longer side facing north (toward the sun). Insulation and summer sun protection with either pergolas or trees that lose their leaves in winter will help keep homes warm in winter and cool in summer.

Water use will be minimized through the use of efficient fixtures and the selection of plant species with low water requirements. After the Olympics, houses will be connected to the site's recycled-water system for toilets and gardens. Non-PVC plumbing and flooring materials were used wherever possible. To improve indoor air quality, low-VOC paints, timber floor finishes, carpet, and insulation were chosen.

Newington Village successfully demonstrates ESD principles that can be readily adopted by the local construction industry and incorporated into new residential developments. The worldwide exposure the Village will receive during the Olympic Games may help to spread these principles and practices even further.

⸺∞⸺

Urban Revitalization and Rural Restoration in Hoeksche Waard

Matthew Taecker, Principal

Calthorpe Associates
739 Allston Way
Berkeley, CA 94710
www.calthorpe.com

What is the proper future for rural lands at the edge of an expanding metropolis, in the face of waning market support for agriculture and waxing demand for new housing and economic expansion? Calthorpe Associates was one of several firms asked by Architecture Rotterdam International (a Dutch think tank for urban issues) to consider the future of Hoeksche Waard, a large island south of Rotterdam that had been "reclaimed" from the delta where the Rhine River meets the North Sea. This was a visionary assignment, carried out over only a few months and accompanied by displays and debates intended to focus attention on regional growth and finding an appropriate relationship between city and countryside.

We saw this project as an opportunity to seek a more sustainable relationship between human settlement, agriculture, and nature. We sought to explore the inherent characteristics within and among these systems and attempted to find patterns that nurture the positive interrelationships that move all systems toward a "mature ecology."

Toward an Optimal Equilibrium

As an ecology matures, systems and processes become increasingly interwoven and advance toward equilibrium. Ecosystems move from a state where a limited number of species thrive toward a mature web in which systems are efficient and optimize resources. The enormous diversity of a mature ecology creates complex interconnections of resource use and reuse that generate a great amount of biomass. "Climax ecologies," as such mature ecologies are known, are also more stable because their interwoven activities are more resilient to disturbances—their diversity offers a variety of robust responses.

The same proposition is true for human settlement. Systems and activities that are better integrated are necessary for an efficient and sustainable metropolis. Sprawling new growth is heavily reliant on a limited number of systems. Auto use and its infrastructure support a monoculture of single-family homes and big-box retail centers.

By contrast, mature urban neighborhoods offer a range of housing opportunities and daily conveniences in a pattern that supports walking and transit for most trips. Neighborhoods with a mix of complementary uses within a 10-minute walk grew naturally before the advent of the car and addressed daily needs, human comfort, and social development.

Unlike natural ecosystems, the man-made environment need not rely on incremental steps to reach a more advanced state. We organize our daily lives and culture to maximize benefits in an innumerable array of enterprises. Yet shaping our communities and regions has remained piecemeal. Developers and transportation engineers have become de facto city builders, though they generally have little vision of how to make communities that operate well in multiple dimensions.

The Importance of Recognizing Place

Integrating systems and recognizing the inherent assets and limitations of a location are necessary for fostering a sustainable region. Calthorpe Associates applied this principle to the Hoeksche Waard, on the Rhine Delta.

The Rhine Delta represents an exceptional ecosystem, where seawater mixes with nutrients washed downstream and extensive tidal marshlands sustain diverse flora and fauna—including enormous flocks of migratory birds. This rich ecosystem sustained original settlement through fishing and agriculture. But the water also conveyed commerce, and commerce begat industrialization.

In time, the region's human environment became increasingly isolated from the natural world. After the heavy bombing of Rotterdam during the Second World War, the city remade itself as a modern or "late-industrial" city of arterial highways, apartment blocks, and segregated land uses. Today, Rotterdam's unique position—the point where the industrialized Rhineland meets the North Sea—has made it a global "gateway" to the European Union and one of the world's largest ports.

While for centuries urbanization remained contained along the paths of barges and, later, trains, the advent of the car and big rig brought enormous expanses of rural lands within the everyday range of commuters and industry. Consequently, the Rhine Delta is being increasingly encroached upon and could conceivably become—with the ballooning potential of capital and technology—a sprawling megalopolis from Amsterdam to Antwerp.

During the seventeenth and eighteenth centuries, to support a growing urban population, the Delta's marshlands were "reclaimed" as polders—farmlands below sea level and protected by Holland's ubiquitous dikes. When proximity to urban markets mattered, these farms flourished. But considerable resources were required to build, maintain, and manage the artificially dry landscape. Today, these conventional farms compete with goods transported cheaply from large farms in Eastern Europe, and pressures for suburban development have mounted. These are presently held in check by national planners, who meter out small, discrete areas for new growth. Pressed now by the Port of Rotterdam for new expressways and land for port-related industries, these planners are now considering a southerly expansion.

The area is also threatened by global warming, which is a danger not so much because of a rising sea level (just build a taller dike), but because more frequent and intense storms within the watershed will cause severe flooding. The polderization and channelization of the delta exacerbates such floods.

In response to this setting and these social, industrial, and environmental forces, Calthorpe Associates proposed four fundamental interventions to shift the relationships among urban, agricultural, and natural systems toward a more sustainable state: To refocus urban growth, reclaim underutilized urban land, make human-scaled neighborhoods the building block for the region, and shape rural land and activities to correspond with the land's inherent natural and locational advantages.

For cities and towns, containing growth and strengthening existing neighborhoods are essential to counteract urban decline and the loss of farmlands and green spaces. In rural lands, agriculture must become increasingly diversified and intensive. Wetland aquaculture, lake-front development, organic agriculture, and tourism can be integrated to protect the environment, create new economic opportunity, and bring the "good life" to the region's residents.

Refocus urban growth. Highway-dependent systems of urban expansion—such as sprawling suburbs—are an inefficient, resource-intensive mode for moving people. They also decant economic activity to the edge of regions and reduce our ability to maintain compact neighborhoods that support walking and public transit. We proposed the containment of urbanization by establishing an Urban Growth Boundary at the Oud Maas River—a natural edge just south of recent development.

Developing sites close in to urbanized Rotterdam will also avoid the need for expensive river crossings and highway extensions and preserve open space. "Leapfrogging" into rural areas forces an absolute reliance on cars and trucks that ignites a familiar cycle of highway building and conflagrations of still more development.

Reclaim underutilized urban land. We proposed the reclamation and remediation of districts within Rotterdam through redevelopment, intensification, the utilization of transit, and the integration of complementary uses at the walkable scale of a neighborhood. Growth should be harnessed to revitalize existing neighborhoods and remake underutilized lands. This process of urban maturation has its parallel in nature, where succession leads to ever more resilient and efficient webs of relationships.

With an Urban Growth Boundary, the economic equilibrium of the region shifts in healthful ways. Industrial blight is transformed into active mixed-use districts. Dysfunctional building stock is replaced. The "leftover" spaces of the modern city are put to use. The parking lots and excessive building setbacks of the immature city can be redeveloped to support pedestrian connections and urban vitality.

Make human-scaled neighborhoods the building blocks for the region. That we have feet is an obvious truth that is too often forgotten in our search for solutions. The modernism of the twentieth century has diminished the livability of cities by forgetting the natural range of a person. Our reliance on the car has grown as we have segregated our homes from the places where we work, shop, and play. Walking can be encouraged when shops, day care, and other conveniences are located within a short distance from most homes and jobs. If built at sufficient density, this mixed-use pattern supports transit service as well.

Our need for safety and comfort has often been ignored. Modern buildings stand as islands in a sea of grass or parking, making streets feel desolate and separating citizens from the city and one another. In livable neighborhoods, streets are lined with windows (and people behind them) that create a protected environment and support daily social exchanges that are immediate and innate.

Shape rural land and activities to correspond with the land's inherent natural and locational advantages. As is true in many places around the world, the farm economy of the Rhine Delta is in decline. The man-made polders that were once needed for growing vegetables within a short distance of Rotterdam are an anachronism.

The solution for bringing sustainable activities to the area is to remake much of the land as it once was—a rich system of estuaries with waterfront settlements. In the maturing region—as in a mature ecology—features inherent to a location are fully exploited. By restoring man-made farmlands as wetland estuaries, diverse activities unique to this setting can be supported. Fish farming and ranching, tourism, and waterfront development are made viable, and they better position these rural lands for the market realities of the new century.

Wetlands can also create new opportunities for revitalizing the flagging economies of Hoeksche Waard's rural towns. Lakes and marshlands are unique scenic and recreational assets that can attract new residents and businesses and allow the towns to remake themselves into "seaside villages"—once the historic pattern of settlement in Holland. New wetlands can also help protect the future of these towns by mitigating the increased flooding and storm surges expected from global warming.

The Maturing Region

In the twenty-first century, urban and rural systems will need to shift toward sustainable practices that use resources efficiently and ecologically. The mature region will become an integrated landscape where connections among systems will be many and distinctions between them will be blurred. For the Hoeksche Waard and other places in transition, holistic solutions will acknowledge the inherent limitations of place and human conditions. Economies tied to local ecosystems and traditional forms of community—where daily needs can be reached on foot—will serve as important building blocks. The twinned goal of urban revitalization and rural restoration illustrates this principle and offers tangible evidence of a region's advance toward an optimal equilibrium.

Eco-Industrial Developments

*Mary Schlarb, Program Manager, and
Ed Cohen-Rosenthal, Director*

Cornell Work and Environment Initiative
Cornell University Center for the Environment
105 Rice Hall
Ithaca, NY 14853
www.cfe.cornell.edu/wei

C ommunities, governments, and industrial developers all over the world are adopting an innovative approach to sustainable community and economic development called "eco-industrial development." This new model, exemplified by eco-industrial parks (EIPs), fosters the networked sharing of resources to reduce pollution and waste, while increasing business success and community prosperity. Eco-industrial development is about changing the way we design, build, and manage industrial systems and spaces to cultivate ecology, economy, and community. It shatters the common perception that economic growth is incompatible with environmental improvement and community enrichment and instead seeks areas where the three interact for mutual benefit. Communities of enterprises, together with local institutions, devise ways to share information, materials, infrastructure, energy, water, and natural habitat wisely and economically.

Eco-industrial development is built upon three overlapping strategies: applying ecological principles to work and workplace design, promoting business networks, and building strong linkages to local community.

Applying ecological principles to built environments and human systems falls within the realm of industrial ecology. Put simply, industrial ecology describes a system where one industry's waste products (outputs) become another's raw materials (inputs). Nature, with its efficient use of chemical resources, is the model for this. A tree absorbs nitrogen from the soil, then replenishes that supply when its leaves fall to the ground and are broken down by other organisms into nitrogen and other chemicals. Such nutrient cycling creates a "closed loop" system that keeps waste to a minimum. The eco-industrial approach similarly strives for the most efficient use of finite resources through maximum reuse and recycling of materials, sharing of infrastructure and services, and incorporating energy-efficient, renewable energy and other "green" technologies into the design of buildings and manufacturing facilities. The capture and exchange of materials and energy reduces pollution locally, lowers the costs of transit, and provides raw materials to fuel local growth and employment.

By creating networks of commercial enterprises, firms improve their market and cost advantages while bolstering a local economy's capacity to grow and sustain itself. The network, like an ecosystem, cycles resources (goods, services, money) locally with minimal waste. Firms making these connections may exist on one contiguous property, be located near each other, or they may create a regional network. Through these networks businesses cooperate to build common markets, exchange by-products and other materials, or share human resources, information, transportation, and administrative services. This not only saves on costs, it also allows local dollars and resources to circulate within communities.

Establishing strong connections to local institutions and citizens can improve equity and incorporate local values into economic development and environmental management programs. A number of communities considering eco-industrial development have held large public meetings where local residents and businesses together envision what they want—and don't want—their commerce to look like. This gives stakeholders an opportunity to make their interests clear and the power to incorporate their values into development decisions, building both support and a sense of ownership.

Eco-industrial development offers a distinct set of community and economic advantages conventional developments often fail to achieve. The environment benefits from better resource use and reduced waste. Businesses reap the rewards of higher profits, lower costs, enhanced market image, and higher performance workplaces. Communities see expanded local business opportunities, more and better jobs, improved environmental health, and reduced waste-disposal costs.

What does an eco-industrial development look like? The classic example is the Industrial Symbiosis in Kalundborg, Denmark, one of the world's most sophisticated industrial ecosystems. Industrial Symbiosis is the collaboration between five independent industrial enterprises for mutual economic and environmental benefit. It is based on a series of bilateral commercial agreements on three different kinds of projects: recycling water, exchanging energy at different levels, and recycling waste products. The Aeneas Power Plant, for example, produces a waste stream of steam and heated water. This water warms the tanks of a fish farm, while the steam is used by the municipality for heating and by Novo Nordisk, a pharmaceutical company. Novo Nordisk, in turn, pipes organic sludge waste to farms to use as fertilizer. Annual savings from these types of symbiosis agreements average $15 million.

Eco-industrial development is already taking off in the United States and internationally as communities, agencies, and developers pursue the type of economic and environmental benefits realized in Kalundborg.

In 1994, the President's Council on Sustainable Development created a task force on EIPs as one strategy for building a sustainable economy. Since then, agencies such as the U.S. Environmental Protection Agency, the Economic Development Administration of the U.S. Department of Commerce, the Department of Energy, and others have been exploring the possibilities for EIPs to follow up on these recommendations. The number of communities considering new ways to combine ecological concerns with industrial development grows each year; today, more than 30 communities in the U.S. are actively exploring this new option.

In Cape Charles, Virginia, for example, eco-industrial development is already beginning to demonstrate its promise. The area's high unemployment and a faltering economy spurred local government officials and citizens to come together to create an eco-industrial development plan that commits to profitability while retaining the social and environmental integrity of the area. The result is the Port of Cape Charles Sustainable Technologies Industrial Park, an eco-industrial park fully leased in its first phase of building. The Park currently consists of a flexible multitenant building designed to accommodate a range of light manufacturing firms. The building's public-private management partnership provides a set of codes, covenants, and restrictions to encourage and reward both environmentally sound practices and involvement with the local communities. Currently the Park's tenants are only minimally involved in actual waste exchanges; however, the management expects this will change as new firms take advantage of special incentives for networking between businesses on-site and with people and businesses in the surrounding community.

Another effort is taking place in an economically disadvantaged neighborhood of Minneapolis. A group of citizens there concerned about the social and environmental implications of a proposed waste site established the Green Institute to oversee alternative eco-industrial networking projects. Seeking an alternative to turning the neighborhood into a dump, the Green Institute built the Phillips Eco-Enterprise Center (PEEC), a commercial facility for high-growth, innovative businesses making products and services to help restore the environment. The Center turned one of the neighborhood's greatest safety and aesthetic issues, the existence of many old, abandoned buildings, into a community asset by forming the ReUse Center and DeConstruction Services. The Center harvests valuable building materials from condemned sites and sells them at its retail store. The Institute is looking for other recycling and exchange opportunities among the tenants, off-site businesses, and the local community. The PEEC building has won awards for its sustainable design features, which pay special attention to occupant health and energy and material efficiency. For example, the building cuts energy use by about 55 percent through a geo-exchange heating and cooling system, and has 100 percent daylighting for all workstations.

In contrast to the Cape Charles and Minneapolis cases, which try to spur responsible growth, the Town of Londonderry, New Hampshire, is using eco-industrial development to address the other side of economic development: how to limit the negative effects of too-rapid growth. Londonderry has become one of New Hampshire's fastest-growing communities, and residents there have mobilized to preserve the town's agricultural heritage and promote environmentally and culturally appropriate development. One outcome of this effort is the Londonderry Ecological Industrial Park, a prime example of eco-industrial synergy in the U.S. One tenant of the Park, a plastics recycling company, purchases waste plastic from Stonyfield Farms Yogurt, an environmentally conscious, socially responsible firm adjacent to the Park. The Park has also attracted AES, a power company that will develop a 720 megawatt combined-cycle natural gas power plant for the site and will use treated wastewater pumped from the City of Manchester's Waste Water Treatment Facility. The Park's management has been in discussions with other possible tenants about similar synergies.

Cape Charles, the Green Institute, and Londonderry demonstrate both the promise and challenges of eco-industrial development in the United States. Of the three primary eco-industrial strategies—ecological design, linkages with local community, and business networks—each project has made significant progress in at least two. Each park has successfully integrated community, local government, and business input, with some degree of public oversight, into its design and management plans. They have also pushed the envelope of ecological design of industrial production facilities and workspaces, winning green design awards for innovation and energy and material efficiency.

The most significant challenge to the realization of eco-industrial concepts in the United States, however, has been forging the kinds of environmentally sound and economically efficient business connections found in Kalundborg. Londonderry is probably the most advanced U.S. case in terms of such linkages. The Green Institute, while currently lacking a formal residuals exchange network between its tenants, harvests what was once considered community waste at a profit. Cape Charles has an eye on future business exchanges, but for now is focusing on recruiting environmentally conscious and socially responsible tenants.

What is the prognosis for these and other emerging eco-industrial parks in the United States and abroad? It all depends on our ability to overcome certain cultural, financial, and regulatory barriers to business networking. First, business leaders must recognize that resources and waste repositories are finite, and that environmentally sound production technologies and exchanges can in fact be profitable. This requires research, education, and promotion of the environmental and economic benefits realized by existing eco-industrial systems such as Kalundborg. Second, communities must have the time, financial resources, and political will to go beyond the temptation of quick, easy, and often self-destructive economic development. Finally, government must establish a favorable regulatory environment that reduces participating companies' risks in tying themselves to other firms. If the blossoming eco-industrial efforts in the United States are successful in overcoming these obstacles, a new era of environmentally and socially conscious business will have arrived.

——✸✸✸——

Reclaiming the Commons

Karl Linn, Fellow
American Society of Landscape Architects

Berkeley Community Gardening Collaborative
1608 Acton Street
Berkeley, CA 94702

For many people, the word "commons" brings to mind the communal pastures where medieval villagers grazed their livestock. As mercantilism and industrialization changed economies, cities, and cultures in the eighteenth and nineteenth centuries, these shared lands were privatized and gradually dismantled, sold, and enclosed with fences. Although the "town greens" in the center of cities are often referred to as the commons, they share very little with the historic lands that ensured communal sustenance and survival. They do not contribute to people's livelihood, and are often not easily accessible for most city residents.

More recently, another enclosure has occurred: car traffic has encircled residential neighborhoods, bringing to an end the vibrant social life that had taken place in the streets and on sidewalks, stoops, and porches. The streets that residents once used as an extension of their homes—where they hung out, shared experiences, exchanged information, and watched their children play—have degenerated into mere thoroughfares for automobiles. In some neighborhoods, home owners replaced their stoops and porches with front lawns or gardens that provide a buffer from the noisy, polluting traffic. Fences, hedges, and parked cars now separate houses from one another and isolate residents from their neighbors.

Urban community gardens are the last remnants of the commons. They are vital public spaces, hosting a continuous stream of people. For decades they have infused American cities with flourishing vegetation amidst sterile buildings and streets. And they have attracted large numbers of community-minded people; it is estimated that some 300,000 community gardeners nationwide have transformed trash-strewn vacant lots in residential neighborhoods into green oases. Since gardeners tend to socialize with one another, these oases have become meeting places. Gardeners can spend time with family members, neighbors, and friends, cultivating friendships and community. The garden's common spaces are often equipped with benches, chairs, picnic tables, and barbecues. Vine-covered arbors in some gardens provide shady social settings.

But this last real commons is now threatened with destruction. During the spring of 1999, the community gardening movement made front-page news when the City of New York attempted to auction off the land beneath hundreds of its gardens. The city was in an uproar. Community gardeners and their friends were outraged. Irate citizens wearing flower and vegetable costumes blocked traffic at rush hour. Pete Seeger led a nonviolent demonstration with songs of protest. Thankfully, some salvation came at the very last minute; the day before the auction, the Trust for Public Land and singer Bette Midler came up with $4 million to save 114 gardens from destruction.

But that rescued only a fraction of the city's gardens. Mayor Rudolph Giuliani's administration continues to destroy many community spaces. On February 15, 2000, the 22-year-old Esperanza Garden, an active community gathering place wedged between two apartment buildings in New York City's Lower East Side, was bulldozed by the city, despite tremendous public protest and a court challenge from state attorney general Eliot Spitzer. Some 400 other gardens are currently under threat of demolition as a result of the mayor's policy of selling off city-owned lots to the highest bidder.

The issue that besieges New York confronts cities everywhere. Two dynamic trends in urban development are on a collision course, and the survival of neighborhood community life is at stake. On one side, a growing number of advocates for healthy and livable cities are asserting the need for accessible open space in residential neighborhoods. On the other, city administrators coping with fiscal crises and eager to take advantage of the urban building boom have launched a campaign of privatizing publicly owned lots, even when those lots have been cultivated and used for decades. But if every lot is developed for housing, neighborhoods will be jeopardized. Cities need to learn how to balance the use of vacant lots for revenue-producing development with the need for accessible open space in neighborhoods.

Community gardens usually grow on lots leased to neighborhood groups, some of which have worked the land for more than 30 years. New York City's current crisis demonstrates the fragile hold these groups have on their land. More than 90 percent of community gardens nationwide have been created through temporary leases of city-owned lots.

One way to safeguard land for community gardens is to introduce guidelines to that effect into a city's planning rules Leading the way in this effort is Seattle, which succeeded in incorporating policy recommendations for community gardens into its General Plan—acknowledging that gardens are a valuable and necessary use of open space. In Berkeley, California, guidelines for community gardens have been introduced into the current draft of the city's General Plan. Specifically, the plan specifies the need to "Recognize and encourage community gardens as a high priority use of open space resources, particularly in higher density residential areas."

When people left rural areas and moved into cities, they lost the support that living with an extended family had provided. It's difficult for today's nuclear families and single people living in isolated houses and apartments to cope with the daily demands of city life. Going to work to earn a livelihood, developing a career, raising children, and cultivating a personal and spiritual life can be an overwhelming challenge.

In any city, residential neighborhoods can become an arena for a new kind of extended family living—as long as there are places where people can easily meet face to face, as happens in community garden commons. Neighbors keenly aware of the lack of accessible open space in their city have been inspired to organize and reclaim land that they can share. In working together to reclaim land and design and build their commons, residents have developed a sense of community. As people of all ages work together, they bond as in an extended family, one based not on blood relationships but on friendship, mutual aid, and intergenerational support among neighbors. Just as farmers used to pool their efforts to build a barn, today's urban gardeners are participating in their own kind of barn raising as they build gardens. Together they achieve what each could not do alone. Amidst the hustle and bustle of modern life gardeners are not only growing vegetables and flowers, they are growing community.

For 40 years I have adapted the old American tradition of barn raisings to an urban setting to build community among people through cooperation. Residents of inner cities have come together with volunteer professionals, students, youth teams, social and environmental activists, public officials, and businesspeople to create neighborhood commons, gathering places close to their places of residence.

During the last seven years, we created three community garden commons in north Berkeley, California, through the same process, on city-owned land and land leased to the city by Bay Area Rapid Transit (BART). Many nearby residents live in cramped, landless apartment complexes next to people in private homes separated by fences and hedges.

In the Peralta, Northside, and Karl Linn Community Gardens, works of art intermingle with lush plantings of vegetables and flowers. These gardens feature commons in which workshops and community events take place. The circular commons in the Peralta Community Garden is surrounded by a beautiful Gaudí-esque mosaic-covered bench and colorful plantings of native California plants. The commons in the Karl Linn Community Garden is framed by an intricately hand-crafted arbor, trellis, and bench. These gardens also function as field stations, demonstrating and testing a range of ecofriendly technologies, such as a solar-powered "flow-form" fountain, bamboo trellis, and high temperature compost bin. In the Northside Community Garden, construction of an attractively designed cob tool shed is almost completed. In these community gardens—as well as in New York and across the country—neighbors who were once strangers have become friends.

In a world besieged by racial and ethnic persecution, violence, and wars; bearing witness to the growth of community as people work together in a common effort has been a ray of hope for me, a glimpse of human and social potential.

❄❄❄

PUBLIC WORKS

The New Reichstag

Norman Foster, Chairman

Foster and Partners
Riverside Three
22 Hester Road
London SW11 4AN
England
www.fosterandpartners.com

After the reunification of Germany, when the government decided to move its parliament and capital from Bonn to Berlin and rehouse it in the Reichstag, that historic building became the subject of an open competition. Foster and Partners was one of 14 architects from outside Germany invited to compete; in 1993, after a second round of competition, we were declared the winners.

Our work to transform the Reichstag was rooted in four major issues: a belief in the significance of the Bundestag as one of the world's great democratic forums; a determination to make the process of government in Germany more accessible; an understanding of history as a force that shapes buildings as well as the life of nations; and a passionate commitment to the low-energy, environment-friendly agenda that is fundamental to the architecture of the future.

The German government leads the world in its responsible attitude toward the environment in the encouragement of renewable energy sources. From the outset our aim was to demonstrate, in a structure that represents the pinnacle of German democratic government, the potential for a wholly sustainable public building, environmentally responsible and virtually pollution-free. The design team—Foster and Partners, Kaiser Bautechnik, and Kühn Bauer und Partner, in conjunction with the German government—developed the brief for an energy-efficient building. The European Commission was extremely supportive, contributing financially to the challenge of creating a model for a more sustainable architecture.

In the reconstruction of the Reichstag, we proposed extensive use of natural light and ventilation, together with combined systems of cogeneration and heat recovery. Here the minimum amount of energy achieves the maximum effect at the lowest cost-in-use. Due to its modest energy requirements, the new Reichstag also serves as a local power station, supplying electricity to neighboring buildings.

The Reichstag's new cupola or "lantern" has quickly become a Berlin landmark; within it, two helical ramps take visitors up to a viewing platform high above the plenary chamber, symbolically raising them above the heads of their political representatives.

The cupola is a key component in our light- and energy-saving strategies, and it also communicates the themes that underscore the project: lightness, transparency, permeability, and public access. At the core of the cupola is a "light sculptor," a concave, cone-like form that works like a lighthouse in reverse, using angled mirrors to reflect horizon light into the chamber, while a moving shield tracks the path of the sun to prevent the penetration of solar heat and glare. In winter and at the beginning and end of summer days, when the sun is lower, the shield can be moved aside to allow softer rays of light to dapple the chamber floor. At night, the process is reversed. Artificial light in the chamber is reflected outwards to make the dome glow and to let Berliners know when the Bundestag is sitting.

The cone also plays an important part in the chamber's natural ventilation system: it exhausts warm air high above the ground, through axial fans and heat exchangers that recoup energy from the waste air. Fresh air from outside, drawn in above the west portico, is released through the chamber floor as low-velocity ventilation. It spreads out very slowly in the room and gently rises up. This provides maximum comfort for the occupants and minimizes draughts and noise. Power to drive the chamber's exhaust air ventilation system and the shading device in the dome is generated by 100 solar panel modules with photovoltaic cells on the roof; they provide a peak output of approximately 40 kW.

Manually and automatically controlled windows, combined with secondary outer glazing, allow natural ventilation into most rooms. These double-layered windows comprise an internal, thermally separated glazing system and an outer layer that consists of a protective laminated glass pane with ventilation joints. Between these two layers is a void housing a solar shading device. Between one-half and five times the air volume of a room can be exchanged per hour via this double facade, depending on the weather conditions outside. The double facade also provides a high level of security so that the inner window can remain open whenever required, especially for nighttime cooling.

The fossil-fuel-powered services installed in the Reichstag in the 1960s produced an alarming rate of 7,000 metric tons (about 7,716 tons) of carbon dioxide annually. Heating the Reichstag today by such means would consume enough energy annually to heat the homes of 5,000 people. Berlin can be very hot in summer and very cold in winter, and because of its great thermal mass the Reichstag responds very slowly to changes in temperature, which is both a problem and an opportunity, allowing passive systems of temperature control to be exploited. Using the building's inherent thermal mass, energy can be stored to provide a comfortable base temperature from which active heating or cooling can be "topped up." This method reduces heat load peaks by approximately 30 percent over conventional methods.

We also proposed a radical new energy strategy, using vegetable oil, a wholly renewable biofuel. Refined vegetable oil—made from date palm, rape, or sunflower seeds—can be considered as a form of solar energy since the sun's energy is stored in the plants (biomass). By using this renewable natural fuel, long-term carbon dioxide emissions are considerably reduced, since the plants absorb as much carbon dioxide in their lifetime as is released in their oil's combustion. Burning the oil in a cogenerator to produce electricity is also remarkably clean and efficient when compared to traditional sources of energy. At the Reichstag, this strategy allows a 94 percent reduction in carbon dioxide emission; heating and cooling the building will produce, we estimate, just 440 metric tons (485 tons) of carbon dioxide per year.

Surplus heat generated by the Reichstag's power plant is diverted into a natural aquifer 300 meters (984 feet) below the building, where it can be stored for future use without any impact on the environment at ground level. In winter, stored warm water can be pumped up to heat the building; it is also used to drive an absorption cooling plant—rather like a refrigerator—that produces chilled water. This too is stored below ground and can be pumped back into the building in hot weather to provide cooling via chilled ceilings.

The Reichstag now recycles rather than wastes precious natural resources to produce a comfortable environment in all seasons. In its vision of a public architecture that redresses the ecological balance, providing energy rather than consuming it, lies one of the Reichstag's most intrinsic expressions of optimism. It is an object lesson in sustainability.

High Performance Building and Affordable Housing

*Patty Noonan, Director of Sustainable
Development Initiatives,
New York City Housing Partnership*

*Jon Vogel, Project Manager,
Jonathan Rose & Companies*

New York City Housing Partnership
One Battery Park Plaza, 5th Floor
New York, NY 10004
www.nycp.org

Jonathan Rose & Companies
33 Katonah Avenue
Katonah, NY 10536
www.ahdc.com

Low-income populations have a great deal to gain from the use of green building techniques. In reducing utility bills by as much as 35 percent, these techniques can make a real difference in family budgets. Similarly, the positive health effects of green building can greatly improve their quality of life. At a time when a clear link has been established between poverty and poor health, and when asthma has reached epidemic proportions in some inner-city neighborhoods, the improvements in indoor air quality that green buildings offer become critically important.

There is a widespread but often inaccurate perception that the use of green building techniques inevitably results in higher costs, precluding their use in affordable housing. As a result, the development of green buildings has been limited almost exclusively to the market-rate environment, where costs can be passed on to the consumer or absorbed by the developer. Meanwhile, the population which can benefit most from green building's efficiency and health advantages is overlooked. While building affordable green housing certainly poses challenges, it is clear that they can be overcome with the proper approach.

Developers of affordable housing will generally participate in a green building project only if it has absolutely no effect on the budget or timetable. Because development fees and the income levels of eligible purchasers or tenants are capped, it is impossible for additional costs to be absorbed. And because affordable housing projects can have as many as 15 different sources of financing, developers are often leery of doing anything that they perceive as further complicating a project.

All of these obstacles can be overcome with a proper balance of education and financial incentives. Many housing professionals are unaware of the existence of green building principles, let alone the substantial benefits to human health, the environment, and long-term affordability that they offer. Even with such knowledge, developers, lenders, and homeowners are often unwilling to experiment with new technologies with which they have no previous experience. Some form of financial incentive for these parties may be required for them to make any additional investments. Educating all the involved parties about the real costs and savings of green building will also help. Finally, the creation of successful models of affordable green housing projects is key to bringing rapid change to this area of housing development.

Education

Although housing professionals may respect green efforts, they often view subsidized development of affordable housing as difficult enough without the additional complications of designing, funding, implementing, and tracking green construction techniques. Proponents of green building must address the concerns of all of these parties. For example, developers, lenders, and government partners must be assured that the techniques will not affect timetables, budgets, or marketing. Contractors need to know that installation of green materials will not make their work prohibitively complicated or labor-intensive. Community-based non-profits need to know that the green homes in their communities will be more durable than traditional homes, and at least as easy to maintain. Environmentalists and propo-nents of green building should also enlist the support of public health experts in order to meaningfully propose green building as a solution to asthma and many of the other health problems that plague low-income populations. Perhaps most important, affordable housing advocates, providers, and residents must recognize that the energy and water savings associated with green building dramatically improve long-term affordability. It is safe to assume that the inferior building practices and materials used in some affordable and public housing projects in the past have resulted in low-income residents paying higher utility bills than some of their more affluent counterparts.

The true costs of green building must be emphasized. There are many low-cost techniques that can be used to make a development project more environmentally friendly. These include choosing a site that is transit accessible; reusing existing buildings or building components; orienting buildings to their maximize southern exposure; and clustering buildings to minimize infrastructure costs and damage to the ecosystem. Costs should not increase if a project is properly "value-engineered"—using techniques that save money in one area to permit additional expenditures in another, while positively affecting overall performance. For example, additional money spent on low-e windows and improved insulation can be offset by using a smaller, less expensive HVAC system, which also reduces long-term operating costs.

Financial Incentives

Even if a project is properly value-engineered, though, a truly green project will have additional up-front soft and hard costs over a traditionally designed project. At this point, financial incentives become important. Financial incentives should be identified to subsidize both the soft and hard costs of green building. On the soft cost side, grant monies from private foundations, financial institutions, materials suppliers, and government sponsors can cover the design and tracking fees. The New York State Energy Research and Development Authority (NYSERDA) offers several programs that provide financial assistance for consulting and energy modeling services as well as incentives for implementing energy conservation measures. The U.S. Department of Housing and Urban Development (HUD), Environmental Protection Agency (EPA), and Department of Energy (DOE) also offer assistance and incentives.

Additional hard cost money can be obtained under a variety of programs. In May 2000, New York State enacted the Green Building Tax Credit Program. This tax credit provides the owner of a qualifying green building direct relief from state income taxes in an amount equal to five percent or seven percent of qualifying development costs. NYSERDA and various utilities offer hard cost money for improvements in electric and gas efficiency. Energy-efficient and location-efficient mortgages are available in many parts of the country through state-wide initiatives or through Fannie Mae. These mortgages allow low-income homeowners to qualify for a more expensive home, covering the additional expense of building a green product. Finally, some utilities and financial institutions provide low-interest loans to developers to finance initial hard cost improvements in a building's energy system, which are then repaid from the operating cost savings over time.

In addition to providing funds for additional hard costs, these programs are important because they raise the general level of awareness of green building and help to stimulate the demand for green materials and technology, which will ultimately lower the cost of implementation.

Models

Proponents of green building must provide examples of projects that can be monitored and analyzed for future performance. Even market-rate housing or commercial projects that use green building technologies can provide useful case studies that illustrate the ease of installation of these technologies and their energy and cost savings. By documenting these projects' successes and failures, affordable housing developers can learn useful lessons that will make their own projects more successful.

Several affordable housing projects that utilize green technologies have been recently completed or are in their planning stages. The New York City Housing Partnership, through the generous support of Deutsche Bank, has recently launched the High Performance Building Program, which will incorporate green methods and technologies in several projects in

New York City. Pilot sites include examples of new home construction, multifamily gut rehabilitation, and mixed-use residential/commercial developments. A set of construction specifications and guidelines will be developed to guide future projects. Jonathan Rose & Companies develops affordable and environmentally responsible communities in the Hudson River Valley and the Rocky Mountains using a variety of public and private financing sources. All of its projects revolve around the basic green building principle of developing near existing or planned mass-transit routes. Other models of best practices can be found in the projects designed by Steven Winter Associates and Christine Benedict, AIA.

Incorporating green technologies into affordable housing requires a paradigm shift in the way we measure affordability; it must come to mean more than a subsidized purchase price. It must also mean that low-income residents benefit from reduced operating costs and improved health, and that the homes in which they live properly account for long-term environmental consequences. Clearly, developing green affordable housing is a challenge. But with careful attention to the education of all participants—in terms of both cost and realistic benefits—and with innovative financing, one can bring energy savings and environmentally sensitive techniques to distressed communities.

Sustainable Affordable Housing

Peggy Huchet, Pilot Program Coordinator,
Division of Housing and Community Resources

New Jersey Department of Community Affairs
101 South Broad Street
P.O. Box 806
Trenton, NJ 08625
www.state.nj.us/dca/dhcr/dhcrhome.htm

The Sustainable Development/Affordable Housing Pilot Program is an initiative of the New Jersey Department of Community Affairs (DCA) in collaboration with New Jersey's largest utility, the Public Service Electric and Gas Company (PSE&G). The program is administered by the DCA's Division of Housing and Community Resources. The purpose of the program is to determine how to incorporate sustainable design principles and energy efficiency into affordable housing. Also participating in this effort are the New Jersey Housing and Mortgage Finance Agency, the New Jersey Department of Environmental Protection, the United States Environmental Protection

Agency, the State Energy Office, and the New Jersey Commerce and Economic Growth Commission.

Sustainable development criteria include the many aspects of building that incorporate principles of sound land-use planning, minimize impact on the environment, conserve natural resources, encourage superior building design to enhance the health, safety, and well-being of residents, provide durable, low-maintenance dwellings, and make optimum use of existing infrastructure.

The immediate aim of the pilot project is to solicit creative strategies to produce housing units for low- and moderate-income households that are affordable, can be produced with the application of reasonable amounts of public subsidy, and meet certain sustainable design standards. The larger purpose is to identify approaches to sustainable design that are reliable and can be widely replicated by developers of affordable housing. The DCA will incorporate these strategies into New Jersey's affordable housing funding programs so as to raise building standards and "transform the market" by establishing a higher standard of development.

In November 1998, the DCA published a Request for Proposals seeking housing development teams to design and construct housing that is affordable, highly energy-efficient, and meets certain sustainable development criteria. New construction, substantial rehabilitation, and conversion were eligible activities. The DCA was seeking creative approaches that use a combination of various proven techniques, including consideration of market-ready, state-of-the-art technologies that meet the program goals. Developers were encouraged to team up with professional consultants, planners, architects, and builders experienced in sustainable design.

Applicants were directed to employ specific sustainable design strategies to as great an extent as possible within the constraints of site and cost. These strategies were grouped into four categories: Site and building design that would reduce dependence on automobiles, promote community and security, and foster appreciation of the surrounding environment. Conservation of resources by minimizing waste and using materials that are long-lasting, low-maintenance, resource-efficient, and environmentally responsible. A comprehensive approach to energy and water efficiency through a well-insulated building envelope, sun tempering, high-performance windows, properly sized, efficient heating/cooling systems, efficient lighting and appliances, and water conservation. And health and safety by minimizing indoor pollutants, ensuring proper ventilation, using durable materials, and educating and training residents.

Applications for pilot program funding were due April 1, 1999. Ten proposals were submitted, requesting $9.7 million to produce 572 units. Selection was a two-phase process. From the group of initial submissions, a review team chose nine projects to compete in a second phase by submitting more detailed project designs. At a statewide housing conference on October 13, 1999, eight winning projects were announced. One project was occupied by June 2000, several others anticipate breaking ground in Spring 2000, and the rest should be under construction by the end of the year.

All of the winning projects have broadly addressed the sustainable strategies and integrated many innovative features:

- All developers will recycle materials at the job site.

- All appliances will meet the EPA's Energy Star standards.

- Energy-efficient lighting fixtures will be located according to a project-specific custom design.

- No vinyl siding will be used. In some cases, fiber cement siding is used as an alternative. Several developers will also use fiber cement window frames.

- All water fixtures are high-quality and low-flow. Outdoor plantings are low-maintenance. In some projects, rainwater will be captured in cisterns and used for landscape irrigation.

- Most sites are close to public transportation. Bus shelters are being constructed, as are bike and walking paths and "tot lots."

- Interior finishes will be chosen with health, durability, and environmental factors in mind. Such materials might include low-VOC paints, ceramic tile, certified sustainably harvested wood, linoleum, and Homasote floor sheathing.

- Developers will hold training sessions for maintenance staff and residents detailing the housing's innovative features. They will also provide ample opportunities for easy recycling.

The projects included in the pilot program will receive several types of assistance. The state-financed Balanced Housing Program will furnish subsidy up to $11 million for gap financing to produce affordable housing for low- and moderate-income households, primarily in urban centers. Funds are derived from a portion of the state's realty transfer tax deposited into a dedicated revolving trust fund.

Since 1985, the program has subsidized the production of 15,000 housing units. The PSE&G Energy Efficient Home (EEH) 5 Star Program will give builders financial incentives to offset typical incremental costs of energy-efficiency upgrades. Amounts range from $1,200 to $2,500 per unit. Homes qualify if they use 30 percent less energy for heating, cooling, and water heating than a home meeting the 1993 Model Energy Code of the Council of American Building Officials. Up to $5 million in low-interest single-family mortgages has been committed by the New Jersey Housing and Mortgage Finance Agency.

The New Jersey State Energy Office has committed $200,000 to design and incorporate passive or active solar technologies.

Developers have received ongoing technical assistance and logistical support from the Vermont Energy Investment Corporation of Burlington, Vermont, consultants to PSE&G; Steven Winter Associates of Norwalk, Connecticut, under the Partnership for Advancing Technology in Housing (PATH), a program administered by HUD; and the New Jersey Sustainable Business Office.

Green Building Programs: The San José Experience

Mary Tucker, Green Building Coordinator, Environmental Services Specialist

City of San José—Environmental Services Department
777 North First Street, Suite 300
San José, CA 95112
www.ci.san-jose.ca.us/esd

The City of San José's environmental leadership, policies, and programs are well known for their completeness, innovation, and creativity, and for their emphasis on education. In 1994, the San José City Council adopted a Sustainable City goal to conserve its natural resources for the use of present and future generations as part of the San José 2020 General Plan. In May 1999 the city began to explore policy recommendations and green building opportunities.

Since then, the San José Green Building Program—whose activities range from the development of recommendations to providing education on green building technologies and processes—has been gaining respect and visibility. In particular, participants in the process value the city's effort to work with the building and architectural communities in the development of the program's activities, involving them in a substantial way in the decision-making that will affect their future building and construction efforts.

San José, the third largest city in California, is in the midst of a tremendous construction boom. During the 1997–98 fiscal year, San José's Department of Planning, Building, and Code Enforcement issued a record $1.4 billion in building permits. Residential construction reached record-setting levels that surpassed even those seen during the height of the mid-1980s boom.

Seeing this increase and recognizing the need for working with the local building community to incorporate environmentally sensitive construction practices, the city's Environmental Services Department spearheaded the green building concept. A series of four Green Building Work Group and Mayor's Task Force meetings took place between July 1999 and February 2000. Mailings were sent to various community, business, civic, and environmental organizations within the area. Architects, facility managers, and builders also received notices asking for their voluntary participation to develop green building recommendations for the city council. Articles and notices were placed in various newspapers and email listings. As a result of this outreach, more than

125 volunteers devoted their time and expertise to identifying green building activities that could be conducted in San José.

Members of the Green Building Work Group and Mayor's Task Force prepared a series of recommendations for action that would ensure increased green building activities throughout the city. The recommendations include:

- Establishment of local green building guidelines

- Development of incentives to encourage green building activities

- Development of an awards program to recognize area green buildings and architects

- Establishment of a green building educational program and resource center

- Work with local partners to construct a green building as a showcase and educational center

- Establishment of a construction and demolition debris program

Even though the Green Building Work Group has been in existence only since July 1999, considerable interest in green building activities has already emerged. Several builders, developers, and architects have indicated their desire to showcase a planned or existing building as a "pilot project" that incorporates a variety of green building techniques and materials.

This kind of enthusiasm and commitment can spur others in the city, and elsewhere in California, to build green.

A comment made by one of the Green Building Work Group members illustrates the community's commitment and dedication to ensuring that green building activities happen in San José. When discussing possible actions and recommendations, she stated that the private sector was not looking for government to do it all. Architects, builders, developers, and others, she continued, are also committed to creating green buildings. The private sector will continue to take a leadership role, in partnership with government, to make environmentally responsible buildings and help create a sustainable future for the city.

Public involvement, outreach, and media activities have helped other San José environmental programs succeed. These include the city's Recycling and Waste Management Programs; San José residents have doubled the amount of material they recycle since 1992, recycling on average 1,555 pounds of materials per year. The Clean Bay and Clean Water Programs have seen extensive decreases in pollutants released into the sanitary sewer system because of education and a partnership between the city and the industrial sector. Working with the Silicon Valley Manufacturing Group, the "Slow the Flow" campaign (an education and media effort to reduce water flows to the city's wastewater treatment plant) saw a reduction of 1 million gallons per day. And almost 30,000 ultra-low-flow toilets were installed during the program's first six months.

Implementation of the Green Building Program's recommendations will also be a stakeholder-driven activity. Many of the participants who developed the policy recommendations also indicated their desire to continue to participate in the implementation phase—ensuring that the guidelines that are developed reflect the local community, that the incentives are tailored to its particular needs, and that the educational activities are targeted to the diverse communities within San José.

Involving the community in decision-making is a detailed and time-intensive process that ensures that everyone who will be affected will have an opportunity to participate. These strong community partnerships will help San José's Green Building Program become a highly visible and successful effort.

Smart Buildings in the Public Realm

Hillary Brown, AIA, Assistant Commissioner,
Office of Sustainable Design

New York City Department of Design and Construction
30-30 Thomson Avenue, Room 508
Long Island City, NY 11101
www.ci.nyc.ny.us/buildnyc

The New York City Department of Design and Construction (DDC), the city's primary design and construction agency, expends close to $900 million per year on capital improvements to city facilities. These varied building projects serve agencies providing vital municipal services, from police precincts, correctional facilities, and branch and regional libraries to cultural institutions, day care centers, shelters, and health-care facilities.

As it enters the new century, the City of New York is in a unique position to improve the overall quality and performance of its public buildings. To address energy operating costs (which currently amount to some $400 million annually) and reduce the negative environmental impacts associated with buildings, DDC has initiated the High Performance Building Program, which is dedicated to increasing energy- and resource-efficient, healthy building practices through demonstration projects, policy development, and education.

Economic Development Implications

As a major regional consumer of design and construction services, DDC can encourage markets for renewable energy technologies and green products through its High Performance demonstration projects, thereby mainstreaming sustainable practices while improving the city's balance sheet. Several cultural institutions have already expressed interest in incorporating their buildings' sustainable features into exhibits, helping to educate the public on green practices and technologies. Moreover, attracting green technology businesses to the city will bring new jobs.

New Industry Performance Measurements

Currently, there is limited public awareness of how conventional buildings contribute to long-term environmental degradation and climate change. These under-performing buildings waste energy, water and other natural resources, and human labor, often by simply meeting but failing to exceed building standards and codes. The problem begins with the standards, which rarely take into account the social and environmental cost/benefits of good design —

how efficiently a building uses resources, for example, or how well it supports human indoor activity, both physically and psychologically. By introducing new performance indicators that factor in such "external-ities," DDC is redefining how to measure building performance. These indicators include facility-specific benefits such as reduced energy operating expenses and increased employee performance as well as municipal benefits such as reduced solid waste and potable water conservation.

Institutionalizing High Performance Practices

In April 1999, DDC published the High Performance Building Guidelines, which promote both policy and technical strategies for city agencies, designers, and building operators. This manual sets out common-sense targets for building performance and the necessary tools, references, and technical means to achieve those objectives. The Guidelines identify building actions that are practical and cost-effective today, such as simple building systems and readily available, off-the-shelf materials. They spell out benefits and encourage best practices while striving to overcome many of the traditional barriers to optimizing building design. The Guidelines were authored in-house by the same technical personnel who will have to implement them on future projects. This investment, together with an ongoing in-house training program, will help DDC institutionalize a high level of commitment to the program. To build this support among its private-sector partners, DDC also sought input from non-profit environmental organizations and local architecture firms and contractors.

Pilot Projects, Current and Future

Since 1998, DDC has facilitated a number of major pilot projects—both renovations and new construction—with an aggregate construction value of $264 million. Projects under development include two new branch libraries, one in Queens and one in Brooklyn, that will utilize passive solar design and daylight. A new courthouse, to be constructed by the New York State Dormitory Authority, should significantly reduce energy consumption through its use of daylighting and other efficiency measures. A foster care/training facility being retrofitted into a historically significant building stresses the careful selection of resource-efficient, healthy building materials and energy efficiency. Future High Performance projects will include cultural institutions, day care centers, and correctional facilities, among others.

The High Performance Building Program aims to improve municipal facilities while achieving significant operating savings that can be redirected towards other needs, such as deferred maintenance or program space. Improved daylighting, better indoor air quality, "healthy" materials, and other critical comfort issues will enhance the well-being and efficacy of government workers and public users alike. Carried across the city's large building portfolio, such green practices can also offer important environmental dividends, such as reductions in greenhouse gas emissions, less air and water pollution, resource conservation, and a reduced municipal waste stream.

EnCompass:
Actual Products,
Virtual Tours

Ann Thorpe, Former Program Manager,
King County Commission for Marketing
Recyclable Materials

King County Commission for Marketing Recyclable Materials
201 South Jackson Street, Suite 702
Seattle, WA 98104
dnr.metrokc.gov/market/encompass/index.htm

The Pacific Northwest's reputation for environmental awareness and Seattle's leadership in high technology meet in enCompass, a Web site that profiles buildings and construction products made from recycled materials. Here, developers, architects, and contractors anywhere in the world can take virtual tours of some of the region's most environmentally friendly buildings to see actual products installed and in use. King County, Washington, created enCompass to help build markets for recycled materials, support the region's sustainable building initiatives, and help divert waste from landfills.

Several online catalogs of recycled and environmentally sensitive products already existed. What was missing was an online presence that could inspire confidence in the materials and show what they could become, rather than simply relaying their specifications or selling them. EnCompass does this through virtual tours of buildings in and around King County that incorporate recycled materials, demonstrating the acceptance of these products by well-respected building professionals. Visitors find dozens of pictures and descriptions for a wide range of buildings. EnCompass also delivers an interactive street map for each building.

In-depth profiles of such prominent examples as the Bell Harbor International Conference Center, NW Federal Credit Union's headquarters, and REI's Seattle flagship store catch visitors' eyes and reduce the perception of risk in using recycled-content materials. Developers, contractors, and designers are also encouraged to physically visit these buildings to see the materials firsthand. EnCompass offers contact information for every project, revealing that many local design and construction firms are experienced with recycled-content materials as well as other sustainable building practices.

Professionals with sustainable building experience are in greater and greater demand as green building takes off in the Northwest, prompted by local environmental concerns as well as a new nationwide rating system. (In January 2000, Seattle's mayor, Paul Schell, announced that the city is adopting the United States Green Building Council's new environmental building rating system, LEED, for all new city buildings.) EnCompass helps the local building industry handle this surging interest by providing practical information on recycled-content materials. The site features profiles of 22 categories of recycled-content building materials and products, from asphalt, glass, and paper to compost, countertops, and wallboard. Visitors can learn about the relative cost of these materials, or explore topics such as material processing and levels of recycled content. Each product is linked to projects that have used it, as well as to other Web sites, such as manufacturers' and nonprofit organizations' sites.

Recycling is one small part of the overall practice of sustainable building, which includes everything from land preparation to materials selection. The entire life-cycle of a building contributes to sustainability, from construction to operation and maintenance to demolition. Sustainable or "green" building features energy efficiency, water efficiency, site management, and indoor environmental quality, among other things.

Though recycled materials are only a small part of green building, the projects featured on enCompass illustrate that using recycled materials can be a quick, relatively easy way to get started. The immediate small successes that recycled-content products bring can allow a project team to progress to more challenging aspects of sustainable building. Recycled materials can also serve as icons of sustainable building, representing the whole discipline. Though it may be hard for visitors to REI's flagship store to see or appreciate the building's unique natural ventilation system, they can easily see, touch, and understand the recycled materials used throughout the store.

Those who look closely at enCompass will find that the largest group of buildings with recycled content is publicly owned. Public agencies are entrusted to promote resource conservation, and many are leading the way by building sustainably. The same is true of non-profit organizations and membership cooperatives, such as REI, the Puget Consumers' Cooperative (PCC), and the NW Federal Credit Union. Some large corporations that have many franchise locations, such as McDonald's and Ben and Jerry's, are also adopting sustainable building standards that include recycled-content materials.

These companies' and institutions' buildings stand as examples of how well recycled-content products can work, and how much they can reduce the waste stream. EnCompass greatly broadens the reach of these examples, bringing images, specifications, and analyses of them to architects, contractors, and interested laypeople around the country and the world.

⟳⟳⟳

Sydney 2000: The Northern Water Feature at Homebush Bay

Glenn Allen, ASLA, Principal, and
Gavin McMillan, Senior Associate

Hargreaves Associates
118 Magazine Street
Cambridge, MA 02139
www.hargreaves.com

The redevelopment of Sydney's Homebush Bay for the Sydney 2000 Olympics is one of the largest urban/industrial renewal projects in Australia to date, and it has resulted in an area of exceptional quality. Hargreaves Associates' Master Concept Design for the site focused on environmental rescue—to re-create the landscape for public use as a sporting, commercial, and residential area. One of the major gestures of that reclamation is the use and reuse of water on the site. Central to this is the capturing of the site's stormwater runoff, its storage and cleansing in a series of water quality control ponds and created wetlands, and its reuse in the site's recycled water system. The Northern Water Feature is a key component of this water cycle infrastructure and embodies the water quality goals of the environmentally sustainable development.

The 770-hectare (1,900-acre) Homebush Bay site originally consisted of mudflats and mangrove wetlands. Over the last 100 years, however, the area was largely taken over by landfill and industrial operations, including the State of New South Wales Abattoir, the Newington Landfill, and the State Brick Works. The Master Concept Design (1997) for the site, developed by Hargreaves Associates in association with the Government Architects Design Directorate for the Olympic Co-ordination Authority (OCA), created an Urban Core of 300 hectares (741 acres) of major Olympic venues, exhibition, and commercial facilities united by a major act of place making.

Central to the Master Concept Design are three key design "moves" that give form and coherence to the project's public spaces.

The Red Move is Olympic Plaza, the central urban space. A 9.5-hectare (23.5-acre) open space addresses the major venues and buildings. This paved open space flows seamlessly like a bold carpet over the heart of the public domain, uniting the site and accommodating huge crowds. This is now the heart of Homebush Bay, a civic place of arrival, a place of ceremony and procession, and one of Australia's greatest civic spaces.

The Green Move is a landscape framework of "fingers" and parks that stretch through the site, connecting Olympic Plaza directly to the surrounding Millennium Parklands. Five east-west green fingers, each with its own distinctive character that ranges progressively from the urban to the natural, were developed. In addition, a large, open green park was created as a counterpoint to Olympic Plaza, preserving significant existing stands of eucalyptus and fig trees.

The Blue Move is the use of water on the site, made visible as an ordering element of the urban core. The Fig Grove at the center of the Urban Core and the Northern Water Feature at the north end of Olympic Plaza celebrate the collection, cleansing, and reuse of stormwater runoff while symbolically connecting the site and its systems to the wetlands, creek, and river systems beyond.

Crucial to the Blue Move is the OCA's development of an approach to the management of drainage and stormwater as part of an overall Water Cycle Management Strategy for Homebush Bay. The strategy deals specifically with those aspects of the water cycle related to the generation, treatment, and disposal of stormwater. Its objectives included the facilitation and procurement of the water cycle infrastructure; the implementation of ecologically sustainable guidelines and practices; the use of innovative and technically feasible approaches; and the completion of this infrastructure within the designated time frame and budget.

As part of this effort, Hargreaves Associates brought together a multidisciplinary design team to develop the concept and the design, and undertake the construction of the Northern Water Feature. Critical to the success of the project was addressing a number of significant design challenges, including treating runoff from a 100-hectare catchment of potentially high peak population density, particularly during the Olympics; reducing average annual pollutant export from local catchments prior to discharge into a receiving waterway by 70 to 90 percent; creating new habitats for threatened and endangered species in an area of contaminated soils and landfill reuse; and minimizing the environmental impact on the adjoining Haslams Creek and other sensitive neighboring sites, such as the Royal Australian Showgrounds.

Since the initial formulation of the Drainage and Stormwater Management Strategy, the concepts for stormwater infrastructure and in particular the water quality control ponds to be located at the outlets of the western, eastern, and southern catchments have been refined. The team further developed the strategies and systems as the design transformed the former "western water quality control pond" into the dominant landscape element that is now the Northern Water Feature.

The Northern Water Feature terminates the northern end of Olympic Plaza, stepping down in arcing granite terraces to meet a newly created wetland at the edge of Haslams Creek. Here 10-meter-high arcs of water fan down the terraces, making visible the cleansing through the marsh of the site's stormwater runoff. The challenges of the Stormwater Management Strategy have been met in a newly created freshwater marsh and transformed into an emblem of the environmental strategy of Homebush Bay. The water feature provides a series of curvilinear fingers with a number of open water areas, protruding headlands, and long continuous stretches of aquatic plants.

The primary stormwater quality treatment features of the Northern Water Feature include the creation of a pool and wetland system with a low-permeability clay liner to keep the water separated from the cont-aminated fill and the groundwater beneath. In addition, the feature includes the creation of some of the deepest continuous deflection system (CDS) units ever built to intercept gross pollutants from the catchment. Construction involved the recycling and reuse of highly variable landfill wastes and construction fill and the installation of a deep leachate system using a custom-developed method of installing polyethylene liners. The creation of the wetland included con-struction of a deep inlet pond with open water and fringing macrophytes, with submerged inlets to the inlet pond; the splitting of frequent flows up to approximately a three-month average recurrence interval (ARI) runoff and discharge at the head of the two arms of the inlet pool (to promote water circulation in the inlet pool). It also involved the construction of a deep outlet pool with open water and fringing macrophytes; the rehabilitation of the existing spillway; the reuse of the existing irrigation pumps; the provision to pump "first flush" to the brickpit storage pond for reuse, to recirculate water from the outlet pond to the inlet pond, to supply make-up water to the fountain, and to irrigate the surrounding landscape. Efficient water management necessitated the creation of control structures that enable water levels to be controlled during macrophyte establishment and subsequent maintenance, and the provision of a grassed overflow spillway in the event of severe blockage of the primary outlet spillway during major storm events.

Edge treatment of the wetland pond is primarily vegetated landscape. At the edge, stepped terraces from three to seven meters wide allow progressive establishment of wetland species around the perimeter of the pond. A shallow, 1:50 grade for the bank adjacent to the pond edge addresses issues of public safety and liability by creating a safe gentle transition to deeper open water. The slope also ensures adequate drainage to avoid still areas of water and allow effective mosquito management. Hard edge treatments and geotextiles were incorporated only where necessary for hydraulic reasons. Strategically placed gabions (at and beneath the permanent water level) direct water flows through the system. Soft landscape edge treatments reflect the environmentally sustainable design principles that form the basis of the wetland design and limit the reliance on expensive imported materials. Graded zones of aquatic and terrestrial plants stabilize the water's edge physically, and visually record the environmental processes operating in the ponds. The fluctuating water level and changing habitat describe the moisture gradient from water to land as an educational narrative. This narrative of environment and water cleansing is expanded in a public art installation. In Osmosis, by Ari Purhonen, the color transition of the artwork (from red, through the color spectrum, to violet), perceptible through the decking of a 112-meter-long wetland viewing pier, interprets the water and wetland systems below.

The Northern Water Feature meets its multiple objectives, including storm water quality treatment, aesthetic and landscape roles, and in now a key component of the water cycle infrastructure for Homebush Bay. It is a signal landscape and a construction that has become a memorable urban development project that exemplifies the OCA's goals of environmentally sustainable development.

The permission of the Olympic Co-ordination Authority to outline the Drainage and Stormwater Management Strategy and to discuss the role of the Northern Water Feature in the Water Cycle Management Strategy for Homebush Bay is gratefully acknowledged. The views expressed in the paper are those of the authors and are not necessarily the views of the Authority.

SECTION 4:

HOMES AND SCHOOLS

The Freedom Lawn

Gordon T. Geballe, Ph.D.,
Associate Dean and Lecturer,
and April Reese, M.E.S.,
Environmental Journalist

School of Forestry & Environmental Studies
Yale University
205 Prospect Street
New Haven, CT 06511
www.yale.edu/environment

For the past century, and especially since the suburban boom of the 1950s, lawns have become something of an obsession for American homeowners. About 21 million acres of lawn now define the country's residential landscape, even in places like the Southwest, where the expanses of lush grass are incongruous in the desert environment. Although a verdant swath of cool, green sod has undeniable aesthetic appeal, its non-native grass species often require a small arsenal of products to keep it green and well-groomed. Sales of insecticides, herbicides, mowers, fertilizers, grass seed, sod, and assorted lawn gadgets now amount to $8.5 billion a year, up 34 percent from 1997. And the emphasis on a perfect, green rectangle of grass often leads us to forget that our lawns are part of a larger ecosystem, that ecology is happening right under our feet. All of that preening and sodding and cutting is, in effect, manipulating natural processes.

Meanwhile, runoff of chemicals and fertilizer from residential and commercial lawns pollutes our rivers, lakes, and bays. The U.S. Environmental Protection Agency estimates that 74 million pounds of herbicides, insecticides, and fungicides were applied to residential lawns and gardens in 1997—far more than necessary. Excess fertilizer can wind up in our drinking water, increasing nitrate concentrations and putting populations at greater risk for cancer, birth defects, and nervous system disorders. Approximately 60 percent of the nitrogen applied to lawns ends up in groundwater.

Power mowers add to the tally of the lawn's environmental damages. Fossil fuels burned by gas-powered lawnmowers, trimmers, and other machinery emit harmful pollutants into the air. According to the California Air Resources Board, a power mower emits as much pollution in one hour as a car driven 350 miles. And we quench the lawn's thirst with increasingly scarce water resources. In the West, lawn watering can account for up to 60 percent of urban water use.

In *Redesigning the American Lawn: A Search for Environmental Harmony* (Yale University Press,

1993), F. Herbert Bormann, Diana Balmori, and Gordon Geballe propose that an aesthetically pleasing lawn does not have to be an environmental nightmare. The verdant monoculture of the industrial lawn can be replaced by the Freedom Lawn, a lawn where no water, fertilizer, or pesticide is used. Thus, only plants that are adapted to the local climate, soil, and insects will take root. Clover, partridge berry, and dandelions will share soil nutrients with the usual bluegrass, ryegrass, and fescue to create the grassy expanse that Walt Whitman famously extolled as "the handkerchief of the Lord." The Freedom Lawn requires little time, energy, or money, just an occasional mowing.

To many homeowners, the front yard is a homogeneous square of soil and grass. But the Freedom Lawn, long on letting nature take its course and short on management, reveals the diversity that even a small plot of earth can harbor. Dispersed seeds from nearby plants take root where conditions are right—some in moist areas, some in drier areas. The result is a diverse, thriving patch of local ecology.

Letting the natural diversity of the lawn evolve is good not only for local plant species, but also for the lawn's caretaker. Since Freedom Lawns, with their abundance of plant species, are more resistant to drought and less susceptible to insect pests or disease outbreaks, less time is spent working in the yard.

Universities, businesses, government agencies, and communities throughout the U.S are now adopting the Freedom Lawn. In Milford, Connecticut, a small town on the Long Island Sound, Freedom Lawns vie for suburban space with the usual variety, largely due to the efforts of the Milford Community Freedom Lawn Initiative. The program was created in 1990 by area residents to curb runoff into the sound from chemically enhanced lawns. Milford was soon home to an annual Freedom Lawn competition, which presents awards to homeowners whose lawns minimize environmental harm and maximize biodiversity. Lots of plant species, bird feeders, and gravel driveways are all marks of a winning yard.

Freedom Lawns have taken root in towns across the country, from Milford to Toledo to Seattle. Even the White House has taken steps to implement a less ecologically and economically costly lawn-care regime. Yard by yard, the Freedom Lawn is gaining ground.

—∞∞∞—

House Reclamation: The Sustainable Offspring of Unsustainable Development

G.T. Overholt, Vice President

Sustainable Living, Inc.
2416 Dairyland Road
Chapel Hill, NC 27516
www.sustainableliving.com

Not long ago, my father and I were having a beer on the beach at the annual family reunion. He had worked for "The Man" his entire life, as I liked to chide him, and he recalled how I had once managed to reduce his entire existence into the epithet, "Lifer." While my father could now chuckle at my derisive wit, that one had cut a bit more deeply than I had known. I had meanwhile tasted the corporate world for myself and had further derided it by dropping out. I opened the first "green" store in North Carolina, built the first modern-era straw-bale home in the Southeast, went "off the grid," embraced organic foods, used homeopathic remedies, saved animals, respected women, and ate vegetarian. Hey man, I was changing the world! I was living my princples!!

Here on the beach, some 30 years after I had hung that scarlet "L" on my dad's chest, something in my self-righteous tone triggered a reaction in Dad he had held back all these years. I'll never forget what he said. "You know, Trip, you think you're making such a big difference. You think I wasted my life providing for you children and your mother. You call me a lifer. A LIFER!" he sprayed again, face turning red. "Well, you know those little aerodynamic wind deflectors you see on top of every cargo truck on the highway?" I nodded. "This old Lifer here helped develop those things. And I can tell you those wind deflectors make more of a difference to this world than anything you have done, by far," he said, punching the air with his finger. While I argued with him then, I know now that he was right. His deflectors had saved untold barrels of oil.

Two years ago, you could fit all of the organic, recycled, ethically manufactured wares I sold out of my green store in an entire year into a medium-size truck. That has now changed. Today, my partner and I are keeping thousands of tons of houses out of the county landfills while we reduce a nearly equal amount of virgin materials needed to produce new housing. Furthermore, while I could not provide for my family selling feminist diaries on 100 percent post-consumer paper, we are doing rather well selling, renovating, and renting homes we have reclaimed. The ironic paradox in all of this is that our company is able to provide society this incredibly sustainable service only by feeding off the incredibly unsustainable world around it.

House reclamation is a great business for so many reasons it makes the hair on the back of my neck stand up. It's good for the environment: trees saved, landfills left unfilled, tons of synthetic building materials not produced. It is redeeming socially: short of single- and double-wide trailers, which are poor long-term investments, reclaimed houses are the only thing that can compete with modular housing in terms of affordability. And unlike modular homes, which cast a pall of blandness on the land, old homes have soul and character and are a link to a community's past. House reclamation is so wonderful financially I hesitate to talk of it lest I create competition.

But chances are that will not happen any time soon. A variety of factors must be present to succeed in the house reclamation business. First of all, you have to live in an area undergoing dynamic development. We are blessed and cursed with it (mostly cursed from my point of view) here in The Triangle, the high-tech and research-fueled growth area encompassing Raleigh, Durham, and Chapel Hill, North Carolina.

Development makes houses available to us through road building (houses taken by eminent domain); new residential construction (developers need us to remove old homes on pricey land they need to grade right away); rezoning (residential to commercial); upscaling (someone wants a sweeter house on the same lot); and condemnations (inner cities die while the 'burbs go up).

Second, you must have several hundred thousand dollars of capital behind you to purchase, move, renovate, and sell reclaimed homes. Often, you have to move several houses at once, with little advance warning. Even if you buy and resell them, you need to be working the business full-time with cash behind you. Third, you need an excellent relationship with several house movers. House moving is a real specialty business. When I think of house movers, I think of Slim Pickens riding the nuclear warhead in "Dr. Strangelove"—they are a different breed and you best not mess with them. Screw up one or two relationships and you can forget about moving any houses any time soon. Fourth, you need a partner— no one person can handle all the details. And finally, you must be comfortable earning a living in ever-shifting sands. House reclamation never gets formulaic like the developments that breed it. Every reclaimed house must be marketed, renovated, sold, or rented in its own special way.

We have a multitiered strategy for success. Unfortunately, we can't lay it all out here, since we hire ourselves out as consultants. But here are our basic rules: (1) We keep the best houses for ourselves. They are the larger, more modern ones, and we move them to more upscale neighborhoods where rental and resale are high. (2) We sell the next-best houses to people who want to develop their own rental properties on land they already own. Sometimes they want a house for the children or the mother-in-law. (3) We keep and rent the lower third of the houses we get and restore them in good, "working-class" rental neighborhoods.

Following these rules has allowed us to build a business that has not only saved many sound buildings threatened with destruction, but has also helped create new homeowners out of people who might otherwise have never had the chance.

———∞∞———

Seventies Solar: A Personal Account

Philippa Whitcomb

Philippa and Harold Whitcomb
290 Solar Way
Aspen, CO 81611

M y husband, Whit, and I live in the high mountains of western Colorado, where we face long, harsh winters and hot, dry summers. We have a scarcity of water and an abundance of sunshine.

As our children grew older and started leaving home, our old house here seemed too big and too wasteful—it didn't take advantage of the sun and it guzzled water and energy. We decided to build a new home that was compact and efficient.

This was in 1977, a time of great excitement in the field of architecture, much of which revolved around solar homes. I accompanied my son on a school field trip to study this innovative approach to building. We looked at the solar homes of Steve Baer in New Mexico; looked at Arcosanti, Paolo Soleri's City of

the Future; and visited Taliesen West, Frank Lloyd
Wright's study center in Arizona. I became enamored
of rubble construction and the rough beauty of
rock and concrete. When I returned to Colorado, I
discussed my travels with John Katzenberger and
Paul Rubin, two teachers who were relatively inexpe-
rienced architects; they agreed to design and build an
energy-efficient home for us.

My husband and I wanted to be involved in the
planning and building of our new house. We began
by mapping out our activities during the day, so we
could have a home that took maximum advantage of
the sun. Thus, the kitchen faces east, to catch the
early morning sun. During the day the sun hits the
living room, and later in the afternoon warms the
children's rooms. The master bedroom is on a second
level that receives sun all day.

We also incorporated a number of water- and
energy-saving innovations. Our arid climate was
addressed by installing low-flow toilets and showers
and the county's first approved graywater system.
This system recycles wastewater from everything
except the toilets and the kitchen sink into a garden
irrigation system. A Trombe wall—an exterior wall
covered in glass, to trap heat that will later be radiated
inside—is punctuated by open spaces to allow sunlight
to stream into the living room. An antique revolving
door reduces the estimated 900 cubic feet of warm air
that rushes in when a traditional exterior door is

opened or closed. A double-sided glass-enclosed fireplace has air intakes that take cold air off the floor and return it heated to the room. Solar collectors heat our hot water.

The house's six-inch-thick exterior walls are poured concrete and rock with a four-inch urethane insulation core in the middle. These rubble walls absorb the sun's heat during the day and release it back into the house in the evening. Whit and I spent months collecting rock by the road, in creek beds, on the mountains. One of the great joys of our 20-odd years living in this house is the beauty of its rock walls and the memories we share of collecting and placing each rock.

We used recycled materials whenever possible. One day we came upon a treasure trove of 12-by-24-inch Italian marble slabs in a salvage yard in Denver, saved from the old U.S. Customs House. (The same marble still graces the floors of the U.S. Mint in Denver.) This marble gave us the mass we needed in the living and dining areas. Our huge 100-year-old fir beams were salvaged from the demolished Swift Packing House; we spent hours with metal detectors removing the old hardware so we could mill the timbers to our specifications. And our revolving door once led into a restaurant in the Tribune Building in Chicago! Living with these materials gives us a sense of history and physical connection to the past.

There are other great advantages to our home. No walls separate the main living areas of the house, allowing free circulation of sun-warmed air. This also ensures that no part of the house feels remote from any other; rooms flow into each other, everything blends into everything else, creating a continuity I don't often feel in other houses. There is a solidness to our home, an evenness of temperature from day into night, from season to season. Additionally, Whit is chemically sensitive, so the wood, marble, and cement floors, the rubble and plaster walls, and the absence of gas appliances provide an environment that is healthy and comfortable for him.

Our "experiment" has resulted in a home in which we take great pride for its beauty, its ease of maintenance, and its contribution to the environment.

Unfortunately, times have changed; over the last three decades, the idealism of the Seventies has degenerated into a philosophy of "More Is Better" and "I'm Worth It." Now bigger and bigger second homes dominate the landscape. In the face of all of this new development, I can only say that living in concert with the environment encourages a sense of integrity and harmony that translates into emotional and physical health, which in turn can translate into healthy communities.

The Hanover House

Marc Rosenbaum, Principal

Energysmiths
P.O. Box 194
Meriden, NH 03770
www.buildinggreen.com/features/mr/

In 1992, I designed a residence for a family in Hanover, New Hampshire; the house was built in 1993–94 and occupied in late October 1994. A systems approach integrating envelope and mechanical system design produced a house that has superb energy performance, yet whose cost did not exceed other custom homes in the area. In the years since, it has proven to be a safe, healthy, comfortable, low-maintenance, and economical home.

All energy supplied to the Hanover House is electric—there are no fossil fuels or biomass fuels used on site. The electric element in the water heater tank supplies all the energy used for heating or domestic hot water. This is sub-metered for the purpose of isolating energy used for back-up heating and hot water.

The principal energy-conservation strategy for the

1,950-square-foot house is a superinsulated building envelope, comprised of R-40 walls, R-60 ceiling, R-11 basement walls, glazing ranging between R-6.7 and R-9, and airtight construction blower-door tested to 0.37 air changes per hour at 50 pascals. Significant direct passive solar gain is augmented by a 360-square-foot active solar thermal drainback system, which is site-built onto the roof, replacing the roofing. Solar-heated water is stored in a 1,200-gallon site-built copper tank. Heat is delivered via a small four-pipe fan coil. The chilled water coil is used to convert solar-heated water to warm air. Back-up heat from a 52-gallon electric water heater is delivered to the heating coil. Cold water make-up to the electric water heater passes through a heat exchanger in the solar storage tank. A pump can circulate domestic hot water through this heat exchanger when the solar storage is hot enough to provide hot water. Ventilation is provided by a Van EE fixed-plate heat recovery ventilator, which supplies fresh air to the heat distribution ductwork. Stale air is exhausted from each of the bathrooms.

In five years of occupancy, back-up heating/hot water has averaged 1,720 kWh per year, costing about $200 annually. This is equivalent to 55 gallons per year of #2 fuel oil at 80 percent efficiency. Total energy consumption for all purposes has averaged 5,083 kWh per year, less than an average home that uses no electric heat or hot water. The house has a full complement of appliances, all electric—washer/dryer, range, dishwasher, etc. Lights are a mix of fluorescent, line voltage halogen, and incandescent. Total energy used per unit area (net) is 10,205 BTU/square foot/year (32.2 kWh/square meter/year). Heat/hot water energy per unit area (net) is 3,453 BTU/square foot/year (10.9 kWh/square meter/year). Thermal comfort is superb, due to the extremely high R-value building envelope and the warm air distribution system that supplies all rooms. Air quality was rigorously protected using the following strategies:

- Source control: we used water-based paints and urethanes; low-formaldehyde-content wood-composite materials; and natural finishes (hardwood, tile, stone, linoleum) instead of synthetics such as carpet and vinyl flooring.

- There is no fuel combustion or storage on site.

- We installed a radon mitigation system utilizing a passive stack.

- Controllable fresh air is delivered to the heating ductwork.

- Efficient filters are used in the warm air system.

This project employs off-the-shelf hardware in innovative ways. The commercial four-pipe fan coil allows the use of a very low approach temperature in heating with the solar-heated water by using the chilled water coil for heat exchange. The house can be heated at design temperature with water of about 100 degrees Fahrenheit. Using the second coil for back-up heat, as a separate hydronic circuit, enables the solar heat and the back-up heat to be used simultaneously, further minimizing the use of back-up heat. Overall, this project used ordinary hardware and technology to achieve non-ordinary results, by careful systems integration.

The Hanover House has required very little operation and maintenance effort. In the first couple of months, a defect which led to a small leak in the storage tank was repaired. There have been no other failures. The only moving parts in the system are the circulators, the fan coil blower, and the blowers in the heat-recovery ventilator. The filters are changed periodically. Controls were designed to be simple. The drain-back solar design eliminates the need for antifreeze in the system, further reducing maintenance common to most solar hydronic systems.

The total cost of the solar/mechanical system was approximately $15,000. The extra costs of superinsulation were estimated at $5,000–$6,000. Total project cost was approximately $200,000, which was typical for a custom house with a high level of finish in Hanover at the time (the house has a fully insulated basement, a two-car garage, and a screen porch in addition to finished living space). The money spent on the solar/mechanical system was similar to what might be spent in a typical custom home in the area on a three-zone oil-fired forced hot water heating system, an EPA-approved woodstove, and a two-flue masonry chimney and hearth, assuming this home also had a central ventilation system. The envelope upgrades are paid for by the reduced energy costs, estimated to be in the range of $600 per year.

A Passive Solar, Straw-Bale School

Laurie Stone, Staff Writer/Project Developer

Solar Energy International
P.O. Box 715
Carbondale, CO 81623

" **A** s the soul gazes at nature it realizes inwardly that not all the demands of vision are being satisfied...but the gaze is bounded and completed when one faces a work of great architecture."

—Rudolph Steiner

Gone are the days of sterile surroundings and square box classrooms. No more stark white walls and fluorescent-light headaches. At least that's true for the Waldorf School students in the Roaring Fork Valley of western Colorado. First through eighth graders there are learning their reading, writing, and arithmetic (along with drama, drawing, and cultural studies) in the cozy confines of a solar-heated, naturally lit school built from bales of straw.

Straw-bale construction has been around for centuries. In Europe, one can find houses built out of straw that are over 200 years old. In the United States, the idea of building straw houses started in the late 1800s in the Nebraska Sandhills area, a region with no trees to use for lumber. Besides being a waste product—it's what's left after grain is harvested—straw is a renewable resource, grown annually. It's also extremely energy efficient. Testing indicates that a two-foot-thick bale has an insulation rating (R-value) that beats a standard wood frame wall insulated with R-19 batts by a factor of nearly three.

The Waldorf education system has been around for a while, too. Founded in 1919 by the Austrian philosopher Rudolph Steiner, the system stresses what's appropriate for kids, not what's easiest to teach. "It's the opposite of today's culture and instant throwaway society," says Jeff Dickinson, the architect of the school. Waldorf's goal is not merely to prepare students for the next phase of learning, but to kindle in them a passion for discovery that will last a lifetime. In constructing a new school, the Waldorf community wanted a building that would reflect this philosophy. Incorporating solar energy and natural building materials like straw-bale seemed a perfect fit.

The school had been renting rooms in an old Aspen school building for seven years. Rent costs were prohibitive, and the majority of families were located about 30 miles down the Roaring Fork Valley. In the fall of 1996, the school board bought 13 acres in Garfield County, four miles east of Carbondale, Colorado. As the school considered what kind of building it wanted, a long list of requirements emerged: natural, energy efficient, light, warm, alive, and earthy. Passive solar straw-bale construction brought together all of these qualities. Building with straw also brought the added benefit of community involvement.

The building process began in the summer of 1996, when Jorge and Michele Sanz-Cordona, an architect and an interior designer, led a seminar on anthroposophic architecture. This kind of architecture, inspired by Rudolph Steiner, fosters spirituality and healing. Dickinson, a straw-bale architect at the firm Energy & Sustainable Design, participated in this seminar. He then began to study Waldorf education and Steiner-inspired architectural principles and consulted with other Waldorf schools and their architects. He soon came up with the plans for the first Waldorf school to be built with straw.

The groundbreaking for the 5,744-square-foot building took place on April 12, 1997. With classes slated to begin on September 2, the entire building had to be up and functioning in just four and a half months, and on a very small budget. Many thought it would never be finished in time. Yet parents, students, teachers, and others from the community came forward to volunteer their expertise. Construction company owners, managers, organizers, carpenters, building officials, financial wizards, and straw-bale aficionados created a team that filled every niche. An ad for volunteers was posted on the Internet and Waldorf advocates from around the world came to volunteer their time. Twelve children from a Waldorf school in Chicago spent two weeks in the Colorado mountains helping with construction. A few of the building elements that required highly skilled labor—excavation, framing, plumbing, and electrical—were subcontracted out. The volunteers did the rest. Sixty people showed up for the wall raising, getting the 800 straw bales up in two days. The school was finished on September 1.

The building hosts five classrooms as well as administrative offices, bathrooms, and ample storage. Each classroom has south-facing windows for passive solar gain, and a light shelf and skylights for natural daylighting. Overhangs and an east-west building orientation prevent overheating and optimize solar gain. The school has hydronic radiant floor back-up heat, and is plumbed for solar hot water collectors. The use of old growth wood was minimized by using Parallam posts, glue-lam beams, truss joists, and prefabricated trusses. The walls in between the classrooms have recycled cotton insulation for sound-proofing. The ceiling is insulated with R-50 recycled fiberglass. The straw-bale walls also act as an excellent sound barrier.

The most striking thing inside the school is the interaction between form, light, and color. None of the classrooms are square. According to anthroposophic architecture, space should respond to the human form, not simply enclose it. The walls are all angled to help the children focus. Natural light is used as often as possible. The building also avoids overly lit rooms, which can lead to an inability to concentrate, and inadequately lit rooms which can cause lethargy.

Different colors also have different effects on people. The younger grades' classrooms are in hues on the warm side of the spectrum, because a young child still lives in a fully open, pictorial consciousness. Once children reach fourth grade, they go through a change that allows them to think in abstract terms. "Cool" colors correspond more aptly to the mood for older children. Lazure Custom Wall Design and New Century Paints provided the organic casein paints and natural pigment washes. The colored paint was applied over a white coat in three very thin washes, with wet brushes and dry brushes, to make the walls feel alive. The white surface behind the lazured color reflects light back through the layers, making the colors seem to come out into the space of the room, not just sit on the walls.

The outdoor environment is also an integral part of Waldorf education. Each classroom has its own entrance to the outdoors. Seven acres of wetlands and river frontage serve as an outdoor classroom and laboratory for environmental education experiences, nature studies, and biodynamic gardening.

Straw-bale construction brings back the days of old-fashioned barn raisings, when an entire community participated in the construction of a neighbor's house. This also helps keep the building costs down. Due to all the volunteer labor, the school was built for only $63 per square foot. Conventional school construction in the area runs approximately $150 per square foot.

The future of the Roaring Fork Valley Waldorf School includes more classroom buildings and a 6,000-square-foot community hall. In 10 years, the school plans to have 20,000 square feet of straw-bale structures on its land. These buildings create an environment that's not only educational but also nurturing. What better environment to put children in than a warm, alive, passive solar structure built with environmentally friendly resources. "Most schools put children in rooms that have no feeling," notes Jeff Dickinson. "With our school we wanted to make a statement while also doing what's best for the kids."

This article originally appeared in slightly different form in *Solar Today Magazine*.

Solar on Schools

John Rountree, AIA, Director

Solar Works, Inc.
130 Compo Road South
Westport, CT 06880
www.solar-works.com

O ur energy choices have major implications on the environment and our economy. We currently rely on oil, gas, and coal—nonrenewable resources that were formed over millions of years. Burning these carbon-based fossil fuels produces air pollution and acid rain, depletes the ozone layer, and is the main contributor to global warming. This last by-product of fossil fuels is already being felt around the world in the form of severe storms, droughts, floods, and unprecedented heat waves. The past 10 years have been the warmest years on record; 1998 was the warmest year ever. The polar ice caps are melting at an alarming rate, making the potential for rising sea levels very real. Heavily populated coastal areas could one day become uninhabitable.

Maintaining our current standard of living into the next century will depend in part on our willingness to shift from carbon-based fuels to clean and abundant renewable sources such as wind, solar, hydrogen, and biomass. Japan and several European countries have already begun investing in these technologies.

One of the most promising renewable energy technologies is photovoltaics (PV). Developed in the 1950s for the U.S. space program, photovoltaic systems now in use in countless applications provide clean power at the point of use. Silicon-based PV cells can provide some or all of a building's electricity, converting sunlight directly into electricity, without pollution, moving parts, or maintenance.

Currently, costs for PV systems are high, but as demand increases prices will drop and eventually solar power will become an option available to all. Education is considered critical to increasing demand; people who are aware of their energy options can take actions that make a difference.

In the interest of educating the public and moving solar technologies to market, Solar Works, Inc., a leading renewable energy services provider since 1980, has initiated the Solar on Schools program. Roof-mounted and "roof-integrated" PV systems are being placed on public and private schools and colleges throughout New England to demonstrate the economic and environmental benefits solar electric systems can provide.

Schools are natural centers for learning and community activity and thus make ideal sites for PV systems. Since the program began in 1998, Solar Works has installed 20 PV systems, ranging from a 300 watt system at an environmental education center in Concord, New Hampshire, to a six kilowatt system at the University of Vermont in Burlington. Educational materials and training on renewable energy are also made available as part of the program. These resources include access to SolarQuest (www.solarquest.com), a Web site that links solar schools across the country; a subscription to Solar Today, CD-ROMs about renewable energy; demonstration PV modules for use in classroom experiments; and a host of interactive classroom and field exercises.

Solar on Schools is intended to create opportunities for students, teachers, and the general public to learn firsthand about the environmental and economic benefits of renewable energy. The program has four primary goals: To teach students about the practical applications of solar and other renewable energy systems through hands-on classroom exercises, Internet activities, seminars, and scientific research projects. To give students and community members opportunities to learn about the economic and environmental benefits of renewable energy resources and how these resources can meet a portion of the region's daily electrical needs. To expand public awareness of the important role of solar energy in controlling global warming and reducing our reliance on nonrenewable fossil fuels. And to link schools, electric utilities, state agencies, environmental groups, and local businesses in partnerships that promote energy efficiency and sustainable development.

Schools wishing to participate in Solar on Schools must demonstrate a strong commitment to educating students and the broader community. Each school must select a coordinator who will become the project champion within their school; identify the role that students will play in utilizing the system; hold at least one public event per year that informs the community about renewable energy; and provide at least $2,000 in matching funds towards the total system cost. These schools must also form partnerships among state energy offices, education departments, private companies, utilities, non-profit foundations, and environmental organizations. Funding usually comes from a combination of these partners as well as from the schools themselves. All contributions are tax deductible through Sunergy, a non-profit subsidiary of Solar Works.

There are similar programs active in more than 25 states. A list of these programs, compiled by the Interstate Renewable Energy Council, is available on their Web site at www.eren.doe.gov/solarschools. These programs also allow schools to participate in the national Million Solar Roofs Program, which was announced by President Clinton in 1997. Any school that installs a 1 kilowatt or larger grid-tied solar system will receive a certificate from the Department of Energy. The goal is to have at least one million solar systems installed on rooftops across America by 2010.

Solar Works' Solar on Schools and similar programs can inspire hope and creativity among a new generation of citizens. Children exposed to solar energy education understand its value and take the message home to their parents. And as they become adults, they will have the information they need to make responsible energy choices.

Practicing
What We Preach

John Schaeffer, CEO,
Real Goods Trading Corporation,
Chairman, Real Goods Institute for Solar Living

Real Goods Institute for Solar Living
P.O. Box 836
Hopland, CA 95449
www.realgoods.com
www.solarliving.org

I started Real Goods in 1978 because I wanted to create a new paradigm, one based on new rules and alternatives to "the system," which I perceived as rampantly overconsumptive and unlikely to survive the test of time. Solar electric systems, energy-efficient appliances, and tools for energy conservation provided people with the means to achieve an independent lifestyle. Real Goods' mission was to promote and sell these goods and technologies far and wide. As the business grew a thousandfold over the next 10 years, to $18 million in annual sales, it became clear that Real Goods was not so much a company that marketed products as one that marketed ideas.

Our slogan—"Knowledge is our most important product"—made us realize that demonstration was the only effective way to teach people about what we sell.

About the same time that we were learning about the benefits of educating our customers through demonstrations, the inherent hypocrisy of what we were doing began to surface. We were preaching the gospel of solar systems and energy conservation, yet using fossil-fueled utility company power, driving gas-guzzling cars to work, wasting water—in short, failing to "walk our talk" at almost every turn. But we also realized that we had the power to make our dreams come true. It was high time to build a place where we could put into practice everything that we had been preaching in our catalogs for years.

In early 1993, we began the process of building the Solar Living Center, a demonstration center for our products, technologies, and beliefs. With a second direct public offering of stock to our customers, we soon raised $3.6 million. Soon after that, one of our employees found our site: a desolate, ravaged 12-acre piece of property in the Hopland flood plain that was being used as a dumping ground for highway rubble. The challenge of turning a nearly treeless piece of waste property into an oasis of inspiration was awesome.

My vision for the Center was to create an oasis that was both a sanctuary and a testimony to sustainable building practices, sustainable energy systems, sustainable living, agriculture, and community. I wanted the Center to evoke a feeling of wholeness that would touch and ultimately inspire each and every visitor. We assembled a group of architects and designers to make this vision tangible. Sim Van der Ryn, former State of California architect under Governor Jerry Brown, had worked in ecological design and sustainable architecture for more than 20 years. He and his project architect, David Arkin, seemed to have the best understanding of our purpose. Chris Tebbutt and Stephanie Kotin, an incredible landscape design team, were selected to convert my dream of restoring the site through agricultural plantings into a brilliant landscape plan complete with solar calendars, living structures, waterways, ponds, exotic and native species, wetlands, orchards, and vegetable gardens that would make any gardener drool.

The Solar Living Center's main structure is a 5,000-square-foot showroom built with straw bales and incorporating energy-efficient passive solar design and extensive daylighting. All building materials used were non-toxic, included recycled content, or, in the case of much of the wood, were sustainably harvested. Other on-site buildings, displays, and exhibits provide thought-provoking demonstrations of energy-efficient techniques and technologies and sustainable use of resources. Solar-pumped water flows into beautiful ponds, and the gorgeous landscape features edible food plants and climate zones from around the world.

The Center is entirely powered by wind and solar electric systems; the site is also home to a huge, 132 kW photovoltaic array owned by GPU Solar that provides solar power to GreenMountain.com's renewable energy customers.

The 12-acre demonstration center is run as a learning facility by the Real Goods Institute for Solar Living, a certified 501(c)3 non-profit organization. The Institute believes that education will help bring about the changes in consciousness and human behavior necessary to create an environmentally sustainable future. Through year-round workshops, site tours, and special events for schoolchildren and other groups, the Institute provides inspiration and learning to all who visit.

What we've tried to demonstrate with the Real Goods Solar Living Center is that the principles of sustainability aren't some environmentalists' pipe dreams—they really work. We can build without cutting down trees; we can build with straw and earth, and we can use hemp and other plant fibers for a myriad of functions. We can build commercially without petroleum-laden asphalt parking lots. We can have buildings that don't use one ounce of fossil fuels, powered instead by sunlight and wind. We can have spaces as well lighted as any commercial building on the planet without using even one energy-hogging incandescent light bulb. We can cool without artificial air conditioning and we can heat without guzzling electricity. We can create glorious landscapes without pesticides, producing enough organic food to feed an entire workforce. And we can demonstrate that sustainable building practices don't cost more; in fact they save money in the long run, by attracting more people who are curious and want to learn, by bringing more business, and by keeping employees and customers alike motivated and inspired. It can be done and we all can do it.

Taking the Elective out of Environmental Education

Wendy Talarico, Contributing Editor

Architectural Record
Two Penn Plaza
New York NY 10121
www.architecturalrecord.com

I was recently invited to give a lecture on sustainable design to post-graduate design and architecture students at a college in New York City. The course focused on current design practices and I was, in 90 minutes, to define sustainability, explore recycled products, and explain how architects and their allies, including engineers and interior designers, can take steps to protect the environment.

After the professor introduced me, I said something to the effect of, "Let's start by hearing your definitions of sustainable design." I glanced around the room with that expectant air teachers get when asking a question that's close to rhetorical. Instead of answers,

I was greeted by empty stares and absolute silence. It was as if I'd asked the students to recite the Magna Carta in Latin.

What was wrong here? Aren't college students fervent in their concern for the environment? Hadn't they argued this issue in other classes? I quickly segued to my definition of sustainability. And as the class went on, it became clear that the students were aware of the effects that buildings have on the environment. But their knowledge was tentative and offhand, a by-product of their education, rather than a focus of it. They knew, for example, what photovoltaics are and that they lower the demand for utility-generated power. But when I asked if they could design a building with a photovoltaic array, they looked at each other and laughed. "I know they have to be on the roof, in the sun," one student said.

Buildings do significant environmental damage, both locally and globally. According to the Worldwatch Institute, almost 40 percent of the 7.5 billion tons of raw materials annually extracted from the earth are transformed into the concrete, steel, sheetrock, glass, rubber, and other elements that make our buildings. One quarter of the annual wood harvest is used for construction. And buildings consume about 40 percent of the world's energy production and produce 40 percent of the sulfur dioxide and nitrogen oxides that cause acid rain and smog.

If young architects—as well as budding engineers, contractors, and interior designers—are not educated about these effects, about the sheer volume of raw materials that buildings consume, the earth's resources will be exhausted, and soon. As Marvin Rosenman, AIA, director of Educating Architects for a Sustainable Environment, and Dr. Joseph Bilello, AIA, of Ball State University, write: "After 11,000 years of building to protect ourselves from the environment, the delicate environment must now be protected from us."

Colleges and universities are doing little in the way of preparing future architects to take on the role of protectors. Sustainable design is just not being taught. That's a bold statement, and partially untrue; some schools, such as Ball State and the Georgia Institute of Technology, do produce graduates who are environmentally literate. But overall, young architects are not getting jobs because of their ability to make a graceful, hard-working building that won't poison its inhabitants, use products made with petrochemicals, or merely eke past the model energy codes.

Some of the responsibility for this lies with architectural firms and what they demand of their young hires. If jobs were posted regularly demanding applicants who were proficient in sustainable design—including the principles of passive solar, natural ventilation, and renewable power—and knowledgeable about computer programs such as LEED, Radiance, and DOE II, students might demand these teachings from their institutions. At the same time, if these same architectural firms went to the schools of architecture at Yale, Berkeley, Columbia, and the University of Pennsylvania, for example, and demanded graduates who could propel them over the hurdles of sustainable design, the schools would respond.

Clearly the most difficult feat is to get school administrators to act, with alacrity, to alter their emphasis from one of architecture-as-art to architecture-as-survival. That means changing the curriculum—drastically at some schools. And that kind of change, points out Dr. Anthony Cortese of Second Nature, an environmental education advocacy group, does not come easily in the rarified world of higher education. "Without strong outside influence," he writes, "higher education is not likely to change its direction far enough or fast enough."

New construction brings an opportunity for change and a way for schools to demonstrate a commitment to the environment. The unprecedented growth of college campuses can mean a real project on which architecture students can cut their environmental teeth.

Pressure for change should also come from, and flow to, the teachers. I recently attended a meeting of the Society of Building Science Educators (SBSE), a somewhat forlorn and abandoned group that's been pushing for a greater emphasis in the schools on building science—of which sustainable design is a component—for two decades. Part of the frustration for this group is, frankly, that building science is not that exciting to design students or their teachers. Who wants to learn about or even teach the stack effect when there are art galleries to design? Who wants to run energy calculations on the computer when 3-D models can be made instead? Who cares about the HVAC system when there are all kinds of lovely finishes to apply? It's like prepping a wall before painting it; no one wants to sand and scrape when there are beautiful colors to slather on.

But as this SBSE meeting proved, at least to me, educating about sustainability can be dramatic and controversial. Try a design charrette where the participants need to strive for zero environmental impact. Impossible? Some SBSE members have spurred their students to create buildings that not only have no impact on the Earth, but that also give back to the environment. There are other educators reaching these kinds of heights, but their efforts are in virtual isolation; there is little sharing of these approaches among institutes of higher learning.

As for the students themselves, it's not hard to arouse their interest and passion. They are, by virtue of their age, position, and nature, interested in and passionate about their subject. They are hungry to learn, even if they have to swallow a few dry lumps of building science to get to the more tantalizing servings of environmentalism.

An architect's highest goal is to preserve the health, safety, and welfare of the populace. In fact, in many states it is the department of consumer affairs that issues an architect's license. The weightiness of that responsibility, and its implications, clobbers you over the head when you learn in an ethics class about the failure of the Hyatt Regency Hotel in Kansas City, Missouri, or, less dramatic but perhaps just as frightening, when you see a brand-new, inadequately designed apartment complex sinking in the silt, shedding its roof shingles, or oozing moisture through its wallboard.

Making the built world healthy and safe means considering the implications that each building has on the environment. There's no better time and place to learn this important lesson than in architecture school. It's time to teach the architects of our future that they hold the power to do something that's more than aesthetically brilliant.

Building Dreams:
An Interview With
Samuel Mockbee

Samuel Mockbee, FAIA, J. Streeter Wiatt
Distinguished Professor of Architecture

Mindy Fox, Editor
Earth Pledge Foundation

Auburn University
School of Architecture
104 Dudley Hall
Auburn, AL 36849
www.auburn.edu

Earth Pledge
122 East 38th Street
New York, NY 10016
www.earthpledge.org

S amuel Mockbee, iconoclastic architect and passionate educator, has blurred the line between experimental design and social consciousness. In 1993 he co-founded Auburn University's Rural Studio, an architecture program that brings students to Alabama's Black Belt to build homes for local families. In one of the country's poorest regions,

Mockbee's students use unconventional methods and materials to fill community needs while addressing important environmental issues. The program has met with great success and has garnered considerable national acclaim.

Mockbee is a sixth-generation Mississippian, partner in the firm of Mockbee/Coker, and currently the J. Streeter Wiatt Distinguished Professor of Architecture at Auburn University. He has been practicing architecture since 1977, and in 1989 he was elected to the American Institute of Architects' College of Fellows. He has served as a visiting professor at Harvard University, the University of Virginia, Yale University, and the University of California, Berkeley. Mockbee was awarded a MacArthur Fellowship from the John D. and Catherine T. MacArthur Foundation in 2000.

How would you define sustainable architecture?

Sustainable architecture involves a combination of values: aesthetic, environmental, social, political, and moral. It's about using one's imagination and technical knowledge to engage in a central aspect of the practice—designing and building in harmony with our environment.

The smart architect thinks rationally about a combination of issues including sustainability, durability, longevity, appropriate materials, and sense of place. The challenge is finding the balance between environmental considerations and economic constraints. Consideration must be given to the needs of our communities and the ecosystem that supports them. In order to put sustainable architecture into practice on a broad scale, we must educate architecture students, professionals, and the public. It's a slow process because it requires a value shift.

What was the early impetus of your work in this area?

When I became an architect I hoped to use my creative abilities to challenge the status quo of the profession and improve the surroundings in my community. As my philosophical sense of the profession matured, I realized that sustainability was paramount. My first connection with the social aspects of architecture occurred in the early 1980s. I helped a Catholic nun move about 40 houses out of a flood zone in Canton, Mississippi. In the end there was one family that needed a new house. We built it from scratch using donated labor and recycled materials. Today, my commitment to environmentalism, social work, and architectural education is both personally and professionally motivated.

How did the Rural Studio originate?

The idea originated in 1992 while I was a visiting critic at a Clemson University-owned villa near Genoa, Italy. I liked the concept of young people studying in an environment outside of their element. It occurred to me that setting up a studio in the antebellum South to design and build homes for those in need would be a great twist on a study-abroad program, and surely a foreign experience. I approached D. K. Ruth, the architecture department head at Auburn, with the general concept in 1992. He and I presented the Alabama Power Company with a grant proposal to begin the program. They went for it. In 1993, we set up shop, moving the first 12 students to Hale County, Alabama, one of the poorest areas in the United States. Our first project was a house using hay bales for insulation, for an elderly couple with three grandchildren. Over the next few years, additional homes followed and the smaller projects evolved into larger community projects, including a chapel made out of recycled car tires, a community center using rammed earth, a children's center, a farmer's market, a playground, and an open-air pavilion for social gatherings. We are currently investigating the use of wax-impregnated cardboard to build a house.

It takes a full academic year for the students to complete a house or a large community project. This year we have 16 sophomore students and 12 senior students studying and working at the Rural Studio.

Do the students coming into your program have an understanding of sustainability?

Coming into the program, the students have abstract opinions and preconceived notions about sustainability. At the Rural Studio they are thrust into the reality of an economically depressed community. The extreme social and physical surroundings broaden their perceptions tremendously. Using their creativity, education, and aspirations, they begin to address social and political issues through architecture. Their imaginations become a working muscle. It's quite amazing.

What goals are they working toward achieving while in the program?

The students execute every project designed and built by the Rural Studio. They work through everything, from the research, programming, design, budget, and material selection to all of the sub-contracting work such as structural, electrical, mechanical, finish, carpentry, etc. Additionally, they physically construct the end product. The faculty ensures their decisions are prudent, but the final decisions are left up to the students. Over the last seven years, using donated and discarded materials and engaging their vigorous, inventive minds, the Rural Studio students have completed 17 major projects and many repairs. The experience is very real.

How are the recipients/clients selected and how are they involved?

The students meet initially with the Hale County Department of Human Resources. They are introduced to several families that are in desperate need of housing and must choose the family they feel would best be served by their efforts. It's a pretty rough decision. From here traditional roles are assumed. The architects and clients decide on a program and select a site. Schematic designs that outline any use of innovative materials or methods of construction are presented to the client for approval. Once the budget is reconciled with the design, the students begin building.

How does material selection/collection work?

The students do extensive research on a variety of materials and construction methods and are particularly resourceful when thinking through the material selection process. Visiting junkyards, farms, construction sites, and lumberyards, they are always searching with a critical eye for materials that can be salvaged. One of my favorite examples is of four students who recently built a community center of rammed earth. They used over 90 car windows extracted from a junkyard to form a skylighted wall. The choice proved innovative, imaginative, and truly beautiful.

Are you aware of any other programs similar to yours?

The Rural Studio is the only architecture program that I am aware of that allows the students total immersion in the social and physical needs of the families and communities they are building for. There are programs that have similar elements, but none that involve students leaving a campus to live and work in a rural, economically depressed area. Our students have a chance to greatly broaden their life experience here. The program allows the students to live the myth that an architect can make a difference in the world. This is a unique opportunity in the development of the Citizen Architect.

How does this experience affect the students after they've completed the course?

It is hard to predict exactly how the Rural Studio affects their lives and the profession, but I have to believe that it will have an impact, that as they become architects our students will continue working with people in need. A group of Rural Studio graduates have recently built an affordable house in Nashville. It took them a year to complete, working mostly on weekends. That's one concrete example. But primarily what the Rural Studio does is expose students to the practice of architecture in the truest sense. It shows them that they not only have talent, but they have the authority to use that talent, and it shows them that they can listen to their conscience as easily as they listen to a faculty member.

How can architects integrate themselves into a community?

Generally, architects deal with only the wealthier 10 percent of the population. Consequently, we are isolated from the larger community. If an architect wants to be involved in challenging the status quo, then she or he must participate in the civic lives of their community. The world will not beat a path to our door. But we do have the ability to effect what is happening in our own back yards. When architects are attentive to the social and physical needs of their own communities, the larger world engages. So it starts with being attentive to what's around you and then making a commitment. After all, the role of any artist is to help people see things both as they truly are and as how they can be.

*Are we coming into a time of increased awareness, under-
standing, and activity in this area?*

We're creeping into it gradually. The real epiphany
will take place when the practice of sustainability
becomes economically advantageous to the general
public. When people realize the economic value,
beyond the importance of the long-term environmental
benefits, then sustainable architecture will soar. I'm
optimistic, but it will take continuous effort and proof
of economic validity. In the building industry, the current
economic system at work for bankers, builders,
insurance agents, suppliers, sub-contractors, vendors,
and appraisers is well entrenched. They are not the
ones who are going to make any changes to the status
quo. It's bad enough that environmental issues are
marginalized by the majority of U.S. industrial,
commercial, and entertainment industries for the sake
of financial profit; what I find even more troubling is
that most Americans fail to understand or respond to
the current environmental crisis.

I don't think architects have trouble seeing the
advantages and necessity of sustainable architecture.
The more difficult thing is to get architects to practice
it, even in some small way. It takes effort and lifestyle
change, on our parts and those of our clients, to make
sustainability a reality in our daily lives. Very few
people are willing to make the lifestyle changes that
sustainability requires. That's the hard part. It's a
brick-by-recycled-brick project.

SECTION 5:

PRODUCTS AND MATERIALS

Improving Our Processes and Products

Jon Spector, Director of U.S. Operations

Dornbracht USA, Inc.
1750 Breckinridge Parkway, Suite 510
Duluth, GA 30096
www.dornbracht.com

The evolution of a public policy in most developed nations that takes the environment into consideration has given new perspective to our relentless development and its impact. From a manufacturer's view, a heightened responsibility to the environment must be balanced with the demands of production. By definition, manufacturing generally requires taking our planet's resources and manipulating them to create something new. Raw materials are processed, substantial energy is used, and waste products are created. For a nation to survive, the economic realities of creating employment and wealth are critical, and manufacturing plays an important role in this imperative. The challenge before us then is to modify behavior, both corporate and individual, to seek a positive balance between the requirements of production and the impact of the manufacturing processes.

The Dornbracht facility in Iserlohn, Germany, is a good example of responsible manufacturing. The manufacture of metal goods around Iserlohn—a town in northern Germany nestled amidst sharp hills and strong rivers—is a centuries-old tradition. The town has prospered and now boasts a population of more than 100,000 people. Factories and homes have traditionally been harmonious neighbors here, primarily because most manufacturing processes were of a simple nature. However, as the town and factories expanded, with ever more complex production methods, the ability to maintain a responsible environmental balance has become problematic.

Dornbracht, a leading manufacturer of plumbing fittings and accessories, has enjoyed steady growth over its 50-year history. When the third generation of the Dornbracht family assumed the reins of the company, the influence of the environmental movement and the family's desire to preserve its hometown's quality of life were critical to planning the factory's future. All aspects of the production process were analyzed and a progressive growth plan developed. Dornbracht aggressively implemented these changes, making significant capital investments in a short period of time. A by-product of these actions was that the efficiency of production actually improved. Thus, the return was twofold: a lessening of the effect to the environment and a positive impact on the company's bottom line.

Dornbracht installed new air scrubbers and water-filtration systems that returned air and water cleaner than that taken in. Product packaging was redesigned, utilizing second-generation materials that are dye-free and recyclable. Arrangements with German distributors were made to return (for reuse or recycling) the shipping containers. Supplier agreements were rewritten to ensure the buy-back of milled brass tailings and other materials for reuse. A new plating facility was built utilizing state-of-the-art galvanic computer systems to minimize electrical use and electrolytic chemicals. Office space was reconfigured to take the best advantage of natural light and air circulation. Recycling programs were instituted for office supplies and paper.

An even greater challenge was in the physical design of the products. Dornbracht has long been a design leader, and compromise of this standard was unacceptable. Working with industrial designers, the company strived to combine the principles of design and environmental responsibility. The easiest task was water conservation by the consumer. The redesign of aerators and flow restrictors resulted in significant water savings over the life of the fitting. A more subtle form of pollution—noise—was also addressed. Dornbracht products were reengineered to lessen the sound of internal water flow to reduce noise levels, especially in multiunit dwellings. The primary material used in manufacturing plumbing fittings and bath accessories is brass, which is an alloy of copper, zinc, and minute amounts of lead. The ratios of these components define the quality of the brass for casting, machining, and polishing. There has been a growing recognition that particulates of these metals are leached out into drinking water from the materials used in water-transportation systems (municipal water mains, residential piping, and faucets). These particles create a risk to the consumer and to the general water supply in the form of gray-water waste. Dornbracht installed an innovative pre-leaching system that removes lead and other contaminants from all surfaces within the fitting that contact water. This treatment results in faucets that comply with the strictest standards for lead-free fittings. All other components used in the manufacture are also tested to ensure safe drinking water.

Sustainable architecture is generally defined as the design and construction of energy-efficient and resource-friendly environments. Dornbracht has employed this philosophy by very closely examining one of the materials used in that construction— plumbing fittings. Obviously, quality and design are primary factors in the specification process. An examination of specific products makes us aware that materials can have a positive impact on both architecture and the environment.

Cool Roofs

Wyndham Bearden,
Marketing Communications Manager

American Hydrotech, Inc.
303 East Ohio Street
Chicago, IL 60611
www.hydtrotechusa.com

As many established building practices fall short by any standards of sustainability, the rules of design are being scrutinized, and often rewritten. Low-sloped roofing technology is one area that exemplifies this trend. A successful roof has always been one that makes itself unknown—it contributes to the building by not detracting from it. What was not previously considered, though, was how that "flat" roof—often black-top or gravel-surfaced—detracted from its environment.

Recent research has shown that the black roofs that crowd our cities and suburbs have failed to manage stormwater runoff. In addition, the heat absorbed by these dark roofs during the day and later emitted has caused a noticeable rise in ambient temperature in urban areas, a phenomenon known as the "urban heat island" effect.

Research on the relationship between conventional roofing and stormwater management and urban heat islands is being conducted by NASA, the U.S. Environmental Protection Agency (EPA), and independent agencies. Their findings highlight the need to redefine standard roof design according to sustainable principles.

The Urban Roast

Our cities are cooking, stewing in their own heat. According to recent studies, ambient temperatures in cities have risen two to eight degrees Fahrenheit since the early 1940s. Hotter cities require more power, mostly for cooling; this temperature spike has added annual power costs of approximately $40 billion. The higher temperatures can be attributed in large measure to the heat-absorbing dark hard surfaces (asphalt paving, black-topped roofs, etc.) that dominate the urban landscape. Computer simulation and other research methods have revealed a lucrative cost/benefit ratio to lowering city temperatures by five degrees Fahrenheit; this reduction could result in annual energy savings of $100 million. Urban heat island patterns are remarkably similar from city to city, except for minor variations in geographical and climatological features, so these figures are attracting national attention.

Since hot conditions are conducive to smog, cooler temperatures would also lessen smog-related health-care expenditures. In cities such as Los Angeles, where smog is especially dense, lowering the ambient urban temperature by five degrees Fahrenheit could cut related health costs by $360 million. In addition, cooling the cities would decrease the rate at which pollutants (nitrogen oxides and evaporative organic compounds, specifically) embed into ozone, which is the principal ingredient of smog. The overall effect would be cooler, cleaner air, and a reduced reliance on energy-hungry air conditioning.

Minimizing urban heat islands can be achieved most effectively by increasing the amount of green space in cities. Although some people have recommended light-colored roofs as a solution, since they absorb less heat than dark ones, altering a roof's color does nothing to actively benefit the environment. The only factor that contributes multiple beneficial effects is vegetation, which cools the surrounding air through evapotranspiration while also lowering fossil fuel usage and mitigating smog. Landscaping a roof also benefits owners by enhancing a building's thermal efficiency, adding usable space, and improving aesthetics—all factors that increase property values.

Vegetation also provides intangible, people-oriented benefits, such as its therapeutic contribution—a factor particularly important for hospitals and health-care facilities. Corporate buildings are also benefiting from sustainable design practices. At the Gap's headquarters in San Bruno, California, designed by William McDonough + Partners, worker productivity has risen and absentee rates have dropped. This is due at least in part to some of the building's innovative features such as a green roof, atrium bays to bring in natural light, dimmer lighting, operable windows, and a fresh-air-based exhaust system, among others.

Stormwater Runoff: Threat or Antidote?

In spite of the many advantages of greening our cities, realizing solutions remains a challenge due to the scope of the problems and the amount of money required to solve them. For example, it has been estimated that Los Angeles would need some 10 million trees to mitigate its heat island effect. This is a tall order, especially when one considers that urban heat islands are just one of many issues requiring municipal attention and funding. Another issue on that agenda is stormwater runoff, which, in some cities, is causing potentially irreversible damage to regional ecosystems.

Whether it's from rain or snow, a city's stormwater must be channeled, purified, and detained within massive, expensive systems. The challenges of stormwater management are universal: it must be continually transported to detention and/or purification facilities, and possibly reused. If not, stormwater contaminated with pollutants from city streets and other sources is channeled to natural bodies of water. As these pollutants build up, local ecosystems are harmed, often seriously. In the Pacific Northwest, for example, salmon are suffering because the waterways they inhabit can barely support life.

Understanding the connections between urban rain and wildlife habitat broadens the scope of stormwater management to the animate world, where it ultimately impacts our own lives. In the Pacific Northwest, where salmon fishing feeds people as well as the economy, damage from contaminated stormwater runoff is adversely affecting businessmen, politicians, city bureaucrats, environmentalists, fishermen, and local residents.

The Sustainable Solution

It is ironic that the element most likely to serve as the antidote to urban heat islands—water—poses equally serious dangers to cities and the environment in the form of stormwater runoff. Thus, the question changes from, How do we get rid of this stormwater? to, How can we use this water on site, to better serve the surrounding environment? How can the water that falls on buildings be used to cool the environment as soon as it hits the structure? If this could be achieved, stormwater would not need to be detained or transported, and natural waterways would have little, if any, contact with contaminated runoff.

Given the expenditures triggered by urban heat islands and stormwater runoff, the answers to these questions are likely worth billions of dollars in savings—and incalculable sums in improved environmental conditions and quality of life.

Greening the Roof

In fact, the answer to these questions exists, and its application in Europe dates back several decades, though the concept is fairly new to the United States. Roof gardens help solve the problems of both heat and water, turning a roof into a cooling center rather than a heat sink while also capturing rainwater. Garden roofs have long been built to manage the urban environment in Germany and elsewhere in Europe.

American Hydrotech, an established leader in waterproofing and roofing, has combined its high-performance waterproofing, Monolithic Membrane 6125-EV, with German garden roof technology in the Garden Roof Assembly. The system incorporates root barrier coverage, water retention/drainage, and a system filter. Together, these layers protect the building and nurture vegetation. The system minimizes structural loading and is capable of tolerating freeze/thaw cycles. It can also accommodate a wide variety of soil depths—whether for grasses, trees, recreational space, or even vehicular paving.

The Garden Roof system helps to protect the environment and bolster quality of life by retaining up to 70 percent of stormwater, increasing thermal efficiency, purifying the surrounding air through reoxygenation, mitigating smog, and deadening sound. Garden Roof Assembly components, including the waterproofing membrane, contain recycled raw materials.

In recognition of the many benefits of garden roofs—both intangible and concrete—many German municipalities' building codes support, and in some cases mandate, garden roof construction. In the U.S., our growing awareness of the importance of sustainable design practices has instigated discussions about similar regulations in cities such as Portland, Oregon; Seattle; Chicago; Austin; and Cambridge, Massachusetts. As more systems like the Garden Roof Assembly are installed in this country and research continues to provide new data about their effectiveness, garden roofs may become the new standard for roof design—a norm that would reap benefits for us all.

Making Windows Responsible

Jim Nieboer, Environmental Manager

Pella Corporation
102 Main Street
Pella, IA 50219
www.pella.com

"We recognize our responsibilities as stewards of our natural resources and the environment and will avoid wasteful or harmful disregard of the environmental effects of our operations."(Pella Business Principle #12)
— *Pete Kuyper, founder, Pella Corporation*

A significant part of manufacturing quality wood windows and doors is respecting the materials used to create them. That's why at Pella, we're committed to continually searching for better ways to preserve and responsibly use these precious natural materials. From recycling to replenishing our wood resources to funding local and national environmental programs, it's a stewardship we've proudly practiced since our beginning in 1925.

Pella's commitment to environmental responsibility guides the company in everything it does. "It directly affects the materials and methods that go into every Pella product," says Gary Christensen, the company's president and chief executive officer. "And it assures those who buy and use our windows and doors that they are making a choice for quality and for the earth."

Pella has identified materials, waste elimination, and product performance as three key areas to address when developing environmentally friendly products.

Unlike other products used to manufacture windows—particularly vinyl and aluminum—wood is renewable, recyclable, energy-efficient, biodegradable, non-toxic, and, of course, naturally beautiful. For all of these reasons, wood is Pella's primary manufacturing material.

Pella is committed to the responsible harvest and replenishing of our wood resources. White pine is the company's wood of choice for a number of reasons. Pine's accelerated growth rate allows the growth of new trees to keep up with demand; precious hardwoods—redwood, cherry, teak, and mahogany, for example—take hundreds of years to reach peak harvest age. And pine is readily available in the U.S., where its cost, quality, and supply are stable and predictable. The Federal reforestation program has succeeded in maintaining supply levels of pine comparable to those in 1923.

Pella works with suppliers who practice responsible wood harvesting and fully support the Sustainable

Forest Initiative (SFI). This initiative was introduced in 1995 by the American Forest and Paper Association to develop environmentally sound standards and procedures for the harvesting of forests. We are committed to finding even better ways to secure the preservation of nature's resources. Third-party certification of wood suppliers will provide increased assurance of responsible harvest and replenishment.

Wood offers other advantages. It provides 1,100 times the insulating value of aluminum. In addition, the manufacturing processes for wood products release substantially fewer toxins into the air, water, and soil, than those used for vinyl and aluminum. The manufacture of wood products is also cleaner and consumes less energy—producing one pound of wood product uses about 3,700 BTUs; recycled aluminum uses 20,7000 BTUs per pound, vinyl, 36,500 BTUs, and aluminum from raw bauxite, 103,500 BTUs.

No window can be produced out of 100 percent wood products, so when possible, Pella engineers its products to accommodate recycled materials. For example, approximately 95 percent of the aluminum that goes into exterior sash cladding and up to 30 percent of the aluminum in the extrusion is produced from recycled materials; so is 15 percent of the glass. This does not compromise the product's integrity or long-term durability.

In developing its products, Pella reuses as much of its manufacturing by-product as possible. Pella goes to extraordinary lengths to use wood efficiently. Laser scanning and finger-jointing assures that even the smallest scraps of wood are used. Many of the scrap materials left over from the manufacturing process are recycled. Aluminum cladding scrap is resmelted. Surplus scrap glass is sold to be used in reflective highway coatings and other products. Nearly 100 percent of sawdust is captured for recycling into pressed wood products, pet bedding, and other materials. Pella also recycles scrap screen, stretch wrap, cardboard, paper, and other miscellaneous products.

The Environmental Protection Agency (EPA) asked industries to voluntarily reduce hazardous chemical releases by 50 percent by 1995. Pella sought to surpass that target and began to aggressively implement design and process changes that lowered hazardous chemical releases by more than 60 percent. Recently, the company installed a catalytic oxidizer at two of its Iowa facilities to further reduce potential emissions of VOCs. To protect groundwater resources, Pella has implemented strict guidelines for the disposal of wastes from its plants. All high-energy wastes are recycled for fuel, while low-energy wastes are burned at state-of-the-art incinerators licensed by the EPA.

The window industry has developed standards to help consumers make an informed comparison of the efficiency of various window products. The National Fenestration Rating Council (NFRC) label appears on most standard Pella windows. The NFRC, formed in the late 1980s, is a council of window manufacturers, glass suppliers, and code officials who have joined together to develop standard procedures for testing, certifying, and labeling windows. The rating procedure begins with performance data submitted by window manufacturers. This data is analyzed by a peer review process and then confirmed by independent testing. Two of the measurements that can be found on the NFRC label are a window's SHGC (solar heat gain coefficient) and its U-Value. SHGC indicates the amount of heat that passes through a window or door due to the sun shining on the window or door. The lower the rating, the lower the cooling costs in summer months. The U-value measures how much heat a window lets escape from a home or building, or, in hot climates, how much heat it lets in. The lower the U-value, the better the window is at resisting heat transfer. The less heat transfer through a window, the less a consumer or building owner will pay to heat or cool his or her building or home.

Pella Corporation is also a proud volunteer partner in the U.S. Department of Energy's Energy Star program, which promotes the use of high-efficiency products. The company offers a wide range of products that meet Energy Star requirements for thermal performance as well as Pella's high standards for long-term durability, reliability, and beauty. However, it is important to note that thermal performance (U-value, SHGC) is just one aspect of a window's or door's performance that should be considered when making a purchase decision. Other factors include: structural stability, air and water infiltration ratings, quality, durability, craftsmanship, serviceability, warranty, and, of course, the company's reputation and commitment to the customer.

Just spend a moment in front of a poorly sealed, drafty window, and you'll know why eliminating air infiltration is an important part of a window's ability to keep a building and/or home comfortable and reduce energy bills. Building owners and consumers can be assured that their Pella windows will prevent air infiltration because only Pella factory-tests virtually every standard venting double-hung and casement window for air infiltration. If it doesn't pass, it doesn't ship. This testing procedure is built directly into the manufacturing process.

All Pella windows and doors also meet or exceed DP (design pressure) standards set by the Window and Door Manufacturers Association (WDMA). A window's DP rating is determined by its structural integrity and resistance to wind, plus how well it prevents air and water infiltration. The higher the DP rating, the better the window resists the elements. The Pella casement, for example, meets DP50 performance criteria, which means no structural failures occurred when it was subjected to winds of 173 mph and no water leakage when exposed to 8" of rain per hour in combination with a wind speed of 54 mph.

Pella Between-the-Glass (BTG) blinds—blinds neatly tucked between panes of glass—are beneficial in both commercial and residential environments. Located under glass, these blinds are protected from dust and damage. In schools and hospitals, this can reduce both maintenance and replacement costs. In homes and commercial buildings, the dust accumulation commonly associated with traditional curtains is virtually eliminated—a key benefit to occupants who may be sensitive to dust.

By paying close attention to manufacturing materials, waste elimination, and product performance, Pella Corporation practices environmental stewardship. The company also supports various environmental initiatives—many of which have been nationally recognized. At Pella, environmental stewardship is not just a marketing program; it's the way the company has done business for 75 years, and the way it will do business for years to come.

Sustainable Forest Products

Lewis Buchner, President

VIDA
3775 Bayshore Boulevard
Brisbane, CA 94005
www.4vida.com

As a second-generation furniture craftsman and designer, my livelihood and my family's livelihood is closely linked to wood and trees and forests. Over the years, a kind of debt has been established with them, which I feel an obligation to attempt to repay.

Forests in all parts of the world are in trouble. Even where trees are being replanted, the biodiverse habitats that are a critical part of the planetary ecosystem are in decline. The causes are complex, and mostly linked to increasing human population, but part of the problem is that most consumers of wood products do not demand that they come from a sustainable source.

Marketplaces adapt to demand. If there was no demand for organic produce, there would be no organic farms. If there was no demand for sustainable wood products, then there would be little incentive for the wood products industry to take the extra steps necessary to harvest trees sustainably.

People often ask, "What species should I use? Is oak good or bad?" The answer is, "There are no good or bad species, there is only good or bad forestry." When it comes to sustainable farming techniques, we do not ask if carrots are better than broccoli. We look for the certified organic label on whatever produce we are buying. In the same way, by demanding certified wood products we send a message to the manufacturers, mills, loggers, and forest landowners that sustainability is important.

My company, VIDA, manufactures a line of high-quality office furniture that uses certified wood products. The particleboard core, veneers, and lumber components all come from Forest Stewardship Council-certified forests. The finishes we use are "zero emissions." Our goal is to bring together sophisticated design, state-of-the-art functionality (our furniture has built-in electrical and data access), and value, while integrating sustainable and non-toxic materials to a substantial extent.

Since the company was founded in 1981 (as Architectural Forest Enterprises), we have used certified woods in all kinds of architectural projects. In the architectural panel division of VIDA, we fabricated certified cherry veneer panels for the new terminal at the San Francisco International Airport. This is a wood wall 30 feet high and 700 feet long— one of the largest and most visible applications of certified wood products to date. And the new head-quarters for The Gap, in San Francisco, features our certified maple panels in the lobby.

VIDA sources veneers from slicing mills which are authorized to handle logs from FSC-certified forest sources. These forests are selectively logged under the best practices for sustainable forest management, and audited by a third-party independent certifier.

Almost every person in the world consumes wood, for paper, for housing, for fuel, and for furniture. It is up to each one of us to make wise choices in how we consume the bounty of our forest ecosystems. But it is architects and designers as well as end users who wield one of the most powerful tools to change the way that forests are managed: specifications. The more value that the specifiers and consumers of wood products place on the sustainability of forest ecosystems, and the more they demand that their wood products come only from such sources, the more the sources of supply will shift to healthier, more sustainable forestry.

⟞⟋⟍⟞

Bamtex
Bamboo Flooring

Phillip Ray, Vice President

Mintec Corporation
100 East Pennsylvania Avenue, Suite 210
Towson, MD 21286
www.bamtex.com

B amboo is nature's substitute for beautiful yet endangered rainforest hardwoods. It is just as versatile as wood, yet much easier to grow. In both the tropics and the subtropics, bamboo achieves great height and thickness in a very short time. The mother plant produces new shoots every year, and stems are mature enough to harvest within four or five years. By contrast, oak, cherry, maple, and tropical hardwoods require 30 to 40 years to grow to maturity.

Bamtex is manufactured from a type of timber bamboo that grows in controlled forests in China. The bamboo is cut and milled into long thin strips, which are then treated with boric acid, a non-toxic pest resistant. The strips are then kiln-dried and laminated together into single-ply veneer. Several layers of veneer are compressed together under high pressure to create a multilayer flooring product. This is milled into tongue-and-groove planks, creating Bamtex flooring and paneling products.

Available in both finished and unfinished boards, flooring sizes range from three to five inches wide and 36 to 72 inches long. It comes in two basic colors, natural and carbonated, to provide a lighter or darker appearance, and can be finished on site with polyurethane or stain. Once installed, Bamtex is more stable—it expands less—than most solid wood flooring. And according to the Janka Ball Test, an ASTM Standard, Bamtex is harder than hard maple, cherry, and red oak.

Bamtex has already been selected for numerous commercial and residential projects in the U.S. The developer and residents of the Bank Note Place loft project in Chicago, for example, were impressed with the unique beauty offered by bamboo flooring. In Philadelphia, Bamtex paneling was chosen for the Sheraton Rittenhouse Square Hotel, which was designed to showcase environmental building products, such as low- or zero-emission paints, as well as providing its customers with filtered fresh air.

Although bamboo is not a widely used building material in the U.S., this easily and rapidly renewable resource can provide building products that outperform conventional ones. Since 1996, Mintec Corporation has been offering Bamtex bamboo flooring and paneling products to the U.S., Canadian, European, and South American markets. Bamboo flooring is relatively new to the U.S., but it has been used for many generations throughout Asia with superior results.

⬦⬦⬦

Making Low-VOC Paints

Carl Minchew, Director of Techincal Services

Benjamin Moore & Co.
360 Route 206
P.O. Box 4000
Flanders, NJ 07836
www.benjaminmoore.com

B enjamin Moore has made a long-term commitment to the environment and to the people who manufacture, sell, and use our products. Our efforts to produce quality coatings while ensuring that our products are manufactured and used in an environmentally sensitive manner are ongoing.

One way Benjamin Moore & Co. is taking an active role in developing and implementing solutions to the complex environmental problems we face is by offering products containing lower amounts of volatile organic compounds, or VOCs. Volatile organic compounds are released from many sources, including large and small process industries, commercial transportation, and automobiles. These sources, especially automobiles, are responsible for the majority of VOC emissions. However, VOCs are also used in the manufacture of coatings. Paint and the VOCs they contain are the subject of some individual state legislation and are regulated on a national basis through the U.S. Environmental Protection Agency's Architectural and Industrial Maintenance (AIM) VOC Rule, which was introduced in 1999.

The solvents used in oil or alkyd-based paints, and in much smaller quantities in conventional latex paints, are volatile organic compounds. Generally, paints require a thinner to promote flow and provide the proper consistency. In oil and alklyd paints the thinner is solvent, in latex paints it is water. The small amount of VOCs used in conventional latex paints contribute to flow, ease of application, and good drying properties. Since latex paint represents most of the architectural paint sold in the United States and since it is already low in VOCs, the public is largely unaware of the paint industry's efforts to provide quality products with no adverse impact on the air we breathe.

Benjamin Moore's Pristine EcoSpec is a premium system of professional coatings featuring very low VOCs and minimal odor. It is one of very few commercially available coatings that combine premium performance with state-of-the-art solvent-free technology. These paints have virtually no odor during application, have a very short open time, and dry rapidly. This rapid drying ensures that there is minimal interruption to daily routines; a space can be painted and put back into use within two hours. There is no residual paint smell.

How does a reduction in VOCs help the air we breathe? Research has shown that in the presence of sunlight, VOCs react with nitrogen oxides to form ozone, a major component of smog. By lessening smog, low VOC paints help reduce tree and crop damage and prevent serious health effects.

———∞———

Pretreating Fat, Oil, and Grease

Max Weiss, Remediator Consultant

Jay R. Smith Mfg. Co.
2781 Gunter Park Drive East
Montgomery, AL 36109
www.jrsmith.com

F at, oil, and grease (FOG) from food service establishments and industrial processing facilities are major contributors to blockage and backups in interior drainage systems and city water mains, often causing unpleasant odors, costly pumping of grease interceptors, and, in extreme cases, excavation of drains, traps, and mains.

Historically, storage devices such as grease traps and interceptors (static and automatic, internal and external) have been employed to reduce FOG, to prevent on-site drain blockages, and to reduce downstream accumulations. On-site storage devices that only separate and retain the FOG require emptying and transport of the contents to a proper disposal facility. Manual disposal of accumulated FOG has its own set of problems, as solid waste legislation and regulations mandate proper handling. However, small quantities of FOG removed from gravity devices or coalescing devices frequently find their way to Dumpsters, recycling vats (intended for edible oils only), toilets, floor drains, parking lot sumps, etc. This may constitute "disposal" in the mind of the person charged with cleaning the device, but this is not what is intended in pretreatment and solid waste requirements, and sooner or later we will pay the price for this pollution.

The FOG removed from large buried storage devices is less easily disposed of and its discharge is more controlled; this also leads to higher disposal costs per unit of FOG. In addition, the pipes leading to and from these interceptors are prone to problems related to grease accumulation. Enzymes, caustic compounds (lye), detergents, and hot water temporarily liquefy and transport the contaminants downstream, but the additives become diluted and the water soon cools, allowing coagulation, resulting in blockage and backup.

Our goal is complete eradication of suspended FOG at the source.

A fully engineered pollution reduction and elimination, the Remediator Grease Treatment System is designed to accomplish this task through the use of environmentally safe live bacteria ("Remediator Culture") which have been specially selected and bred to have broad appetites to digest fat, oil, grease, sugar, and starch and other complex carbohydrates and proteins. The Remediator Culture includes nine different strains of natural bacteria which are beneficial, natural, and non-pathogenic (non-infectious). The bacteria is introduced to produce a broad-specie biofilm on the large surface area of the media and the interior of the Remediator. The organisms inhabiting the biofilm reduce the FOG to CO_2 and water.

The Remediator is fundamentally a small-scale fixed film bioreactor which has the added functions of separation and retention of suspended FOG. The separation, retention, and disposal functions are effected through the interactive functions of fluid mechanics and bioremediation within the specially designed media in the Remediator. The system is specifically designed to provide the greatest possible surface area, incorporating a unique honeycomb-type media (patent pending) on which the biofilm (bacteria colony) is maintained. Through applied hydrodynamics, the media separates and retains material in the influent and transfers it to the biofilm within the honeycomb media structure for digestion.

The system incorporates a solids separator that retains food scraps and particles. The Remediator is designed to separate, retain, and dispose of FOG, a liquid pollutant that is not efficiently separated, retained, or easily disposed of by gravity interceptors.

Solid material is not a liquid pollutant and is easily disposed of. The system features that make it extremely efficient at separating and retaining liquid pollutants also make it extremely efficient at separating and retaining solids, a pollutant the Remediator is not designed to digest. Solids require much longer to break down in a biofilm and will accumulate over time, eventually causing odor and partial or complete blockage of the unit, which is why a solids separator is included.

Approximately once a year, residues of silt (from floor drains, scouring agents, etc.) should be removed (using a wet vacuum) from the Remediator. This material can be disposed of in standard fashion of handling solid waste. It is non-toxic and requires no special handling.

This easy-to-install system with no moving parts is the most reasonable solution to the problem of grease pollution. The end result of the natural, environmentally friendly bioremediation process is a high-quality water exiting the device with FOG content below 100 mg/l at 20 to 75 gallons per minute rates, without requiring periodic cleaning or pumping.

This paper consists of excerpts from Jay R. Smith literature and "Pretreating Grease," an article published in the January-February 1999 issue of *PMEngineer* magazine.

—⚬⚭⚬—

Flexible Furniture Systems

Carin Ganz, Marketing Communications Coordinator

Bretford
11000 Seymour Avenue
Franklin Park, IL 60131
www.bretford.com

I n preparation for the turn of the twenty-first century, Bretford sought out ways to make its manufacturing processes more environmentally safe. This effort began in 1985 when the company switched its painting process from a highly VOC-saturated spray-on wet paint to an electrostatic powder paint technology. This switch, combined with the company's participation in the EPA's Emissions Reduction Market System, has allowed Bretford to reduce its seasonal emissions by at least 12 percent. The focus on emissions reduction has also made an impact in the painting processes, manufacturing lines, and power systems at Bretford. The introduction of a new UV finishing line and a solvent cleaning agent has helped reduce emissions of VOCs by almost 60 percent.

Recycling has also become key to Bretford's green efforts. After it is used, the solvent cleaning agent is recycled as part of a fuel blend that powers the company's manufacturing facilities. Wood scraps left over from the manufacturing process are used in energy generators that heat the factory's boilers. A company-wide recycling campaign begun in the 1990s includes separating paper and plastic products, the collection of aluminum cans, and, with the implementation of Lotus Notes, an attempt to create a paper-free workplace.

Recycling isn't Bretford's only green focal point. The company's furniture lines take a caring and humane approach. With the introduction of the Here Metamobile System and Free System, Bretford has created furniture lines that address human well-being.

Here Metamobile Meeting Solutions is a completely modular system, fostering creativity and communication. Transforming the configuration of a room is simple. Here's casters enable the tables to change to serve multiple uses, quickly and with little effort. Users can set tables up individually for separate work centers, link them together with the unique ganging Gere to form conference tables, and, with mobile boards, separate them for group teaming. Work environments move quickly and simply.

The Free System is a flexible series of desks, file cabinets, screens, and power sources that not only grow with an evolving company but also adhere to the physical needs of the employees using them. The

Mini, Multi, and Maxi workstations wrap around the user, bringing phone, paperwork, and computer to his or her fingertips. The workstations adapt to changing needs with entirely height-adjustable work surfaces, monitor stands, and keyboard position. Adjustability enables the system to suit almost anyone. The ergonomically correct form of the furniture helps ensure health and safety in the working environment and reduces work-related conditions such as carpal tunnel syndrome and backaches. Free also promotes the idea of easy reconfiguration for the changing needs of a workspace. Glides promote flexibility in an environment and help reduce costs. With the addition of new employees, it is not necessary to go through the expense of tearing down and rebuilding cubicles. Simply order a new workstation, move the furniture, and a new environment is created. Free's fluid lines and anamorphic shapes fit around any structure and adapt to an office's atmosphere. The Free and Here Systems are responsive to the needs of growing companies and provide users with a friendly and comfortable working environment.

With an active approach towards recycling programs, reducing the emission of toxins, and manufacturing furniture with human health in mind, Bretford Manufacturing demonstrates a unique interest in the natural and work environment.

High-Performance Wire and Cable Management Systems

Don Torrant, Manager,
Marketing Communications

The Wiremold Company
60 Woodlawn Street
West Hartford, CT 06110
www.wiremold.com

W ire and cable management systems contribute to sustainable architecture in several important ways. Without an effective data/communications cabling infrastructure, the useful life of a building is likely to be considerably shorter than that of the materials used in its construction. Inaccessible cabling limits the ability of a building to adapt to new computer and communications technologies. A flexible wire and cable management system makes it possible to keep pace with emerging technologies. In contrast to wiring installed within walls, cables in wire management systems can be easily removed when a data/communications system is upgraded. Instead of leaving outdated cables in walls or above ceilings, valuable copper can be recycled. Wire and cable management systems also facilitate the renovation of existing structures by providing an easy-to-install infrastructure that can support high-performance data/communications cabling. In historical structures, these systems reduce or eliminate the need for extensive (and expensive) wall, ceiling, or floor penetrations.

Unfortunately, there is still a tendency to think of data/communications installations as something that can be slipped into a building moments before the occupants arrive. According to some estimates, 75 percent of workstation wiring and cabling is installed after a new or renovated building is occupied. But achieving the optimal wire and cable system infrastructure requires the active involvement of the design team and building owners throughout the design process. Waiting until late in the design process to consider wire and cable management entails some risks, including:

• Eliminating certain highly effective cabling pathway solutions. Cellular deck and infloor duct systems, for example, must be considered early in the process. Optimal placement of other infrastructure components, such as cable trays, may be impossible if the design does not provide for them.

• Reducing building flexibility. Effective utilization of space depends on the availability of communications technology and ability to reconfigure the space with minimal downtime.

- Failing to consider the impact of future technology. While no one can predict future technologies, a robust, accessible, and adaptable cabling infrastructure is an effective strategy for maintaining a building's long-term function.

- Increasing the costs and difficulty associated with installing and changing the cabling system.

- Encouraging a patchwork of stopgap, unattractive wiring.

In buildings without a well-planned technology infrastructure, designers often specify a high-capacity distribution system, figuring that the added capacity will ensure flexibility. But this may not be a cost-effective long-range solution, and it certainly adds up-front costs. Excessive capacity can also compound design and aesthetic problems. If the solution is not merely adding capacity, then what is it? There are several points to consider before answering.

How many services are needed at each point of use? Typical workstations require five services: filtered, surge-protected, isolated-ground AC power; unfiltered AC power; LAN connection; modem line; and telephone line. A growing number of workstations also need specialized services, such as desktop video.

Is the cabling system going to need to be upgraded to meet future technology? The answer is almost certainly yes. This means accessibility for change-out is essential. The cabling infrastructure must also accommodate the required bend radius of fiber-optic and high-performance copper cable. Make sure the system will have the expected bandwidth and technical performance when needed.

How frequently will it be necessary to move people or add workstations? The cabling infrastructure must be flexible for moves, adds, and changes with minimal downtime.

How much do you want to see? Aesthetic requirements vary from space to space. What is effective in a back office might not be appropriate for a conference room. Investigate which cabling infrastructure components best suit the surrounding space.

Wire and cable management systems can be grouped into five primary categories. In-floor systems include in-floor and cellular duct and raised floor systems. Duct systems provide support and security for cabling in reinforced concrete and steel constructions. Raised floor boxes offer convenient access to data/communications cabling. Open space systems, such as floor boxes and poke-thru devices, serve areas that are not adjacent to partitions. These systems provide direct access to cabling or they can feed into modular office furniture. Installed in core-drilled holes, poke-thru fittings maintain the fire rating of floors. Service poles are another option for open space applications. Perimeter systems route wiring and cabling securely along walls. These systems are often specified for conference rooms, offices, classrooms, laboratories, and training centers. Unlike conventional conduit, cabling in a perimeter system remains easily accessible at all times. These systems are also easy to expand or reconfigure. Overhead systems offer a high degree of flexibility in terms of both locating the components and accessing the cabling within them. Although cable tray was historically installed above drop ceilings, it is increasingly showing up in open ceiling applications. Point-of-use solutions focus on the workstation. Here, the objective is to provide communications connectivity that is compatible with all cabling pathways. Modular systems enable a diverse array of connecting components to be installed in standard face plates or mounting bezels.

The challenge for designers is to maximize building function by meeting current and future space and technology requirements with minimal impact. Central to achieving this is an integral, building-wide infrastructure that distributes data/communications cabling from communications closets to individual workstations. These systems ensure maximum operational and systems flexibility; prolong building life by accommodating any and all data/communications cabling; and enhance aesthetics by concealing wires and cables. These qualities are all important to creating sustainable architecture; adaptability, reduction of waste, and an ability to retrofit existing buildings all reduce the waste stream and help conserve resources, while attractive offices foster well-being among workers.

Durable Furniture

USM Marketing Team, Munsingen, Switzerland

USM Modular Furniture
150 East 58th Street
New York, NY 10155
www.usm.com

S ince the company's inception in the 1960s, one goal of USM Modular Furniture has been to deal with the issues of design, raw materials, production methods, and energy consumption in an environmentally responsible way. As we set out on this task, we also took into consideration the social, economic, and ecological relationships that are fundamental to systems engineering.

We would like to introduce you to our efforts to support the evolution of sustainable design. To begin, we have divided our topic into four sections—Raw Materials, Manufacturing, Utilization, and Disposal— to better analyze the individual elements that can create an ecological balance. Our efforts are not definitive; ecological responsibility is a process that requires constant review.

Raw Materials

- *Structure:* The weight-bearing structure for USM Modular Furniture systems is made of steel. Thanks to its excellent material properties, it guarantees sturdiness and stability.

- *Door elements:* In addition to steel, which is powder-coated in ten lightfast colors, we also use glass as an enclosure material.

- *Table surfaces:* Tabletops consist of granite, glass, laminate boards, or wood veneers (black oak, beech). The wood veneers are produced from European timber. The glue used has an extremely low formaldehyde content and fulfills the requirements of the most stringent E1 Emission Class for the EU and the CH10 Quality Mark for Switzerland.

- *Filing elements:* The internal organizational system is primarily constructed of powder-coated steel. For additional sectioning, polystyrene is used—an already recycled plastic.

- *Composite materials:* With the exception of the laminate boards and the leveling feet, no composite materials are used. This ensures that USM Modular Furniture can be dismantled and efficiently sorted according to recyclable material content, so at the end of their useful lives the individual materials are ready to be reintegrated back into the materials cycle.

Production and Finishing Methods

- *Industrial production:* USM Modular Furniture is produced industrially, in large volumes. High-precision production techniques minimize machine costs, and reduce both energy and resource consumption. Residual production materials are completely recycled.

- *Chromium plating:* Chromium, which is used for coating the exposed steel frame, is extremely wear- and corrosion-resistant and therefore extremely durable. In its metallic form, chromium is completely harmless and is used in many areas of daily life. Chromium does pose an environmental problem in its acidic form, which is still required for the chroming process. The selection of highly specialized electroplating shops that use the latest technology ensures a self-contained chroming cycle. The small amount of chromic acid extracted from the refuse is almost fully recycled.

- *Powder coating:* USM uses up-to-date powder-coating facilities that employ heat recovery and suction units. Environmentally friendly polyurethane powder is applied to the sheets after cleaning and baked at 190 degrees Celsius. No solvents whatsoever are used. Almost all leftover powder is reintroduced back into the materials cycle.

Utilization

From an ecological viewpoint, the most important quality of a product is the length of its useful life. It is an unavoidable fact that every production process consumes energy and resources. It is also true that at some point, the usefulness of a given product has reached its "expiration date," when it must be disposed of. The longer a product is usable, the better for the environment. USM Modular Furniture uses long-lasting materials, including steel tubes and shelves, a lightfast powder coating, an exposed weight-bearing structure in high-gloss chrome, and wood, glass, and granite tabletops.

USM furniture systems are custom-configured for the user's specific needs. If the requirements placed on the furniture systems change due to spatial modifications or client requests, the system can be easily adapted at any time with simple reconfiguring. For example, a filing unit can become a sideboard or stereo/TV cabinet. Most USM Modular Furniture systems produced over the past 25 years are still in use—always effortlessly adaptable to the changing needs of their users.

Recycling and Disposal

Our modular furniture systems are made of primarily recyclable materials. The USM Haller Furniture System, for example, is 97 percent steel, 1.5 percent plastic, and 1.5 percent composite materials. USM Haller Glass Cabinets are 24 percent steel, 75 percent glass, and 1 percent plastic and composite materials.

If reconfiguring the USM product for new functions is impossible, the individual system parts can be sorted and returned to the production cycle. Steel is largely reused. Even powder-coated or chromium-plated parts can be melted down in high-temperature blast furnaces. Glass is a 100 percent recyclable material; our glass works use a high proportion of recycled glass in their production processes. The plastic used, polystyrene, is also 100 percent recyclable. Composite materials are disposed of in incinerators equipped with optimum combustion temperatures in combination with units for flue gas dust collection, ensuring that exhaust gases satisfy clean air regulations.

USM is proud to participate and aid in the development of sustainable architecture through our product design, production techniques, raw materials, and reduced energy consumption.

—————∞∞∞—————

The Recycled Office

Gary M. Petersen, Partner

Environmental Problem Solving Enterprises
528 Arizona Avenue, Suite 209
Santa Monica, CA 90401
www.epse.net

I confess. I'm a longhair, a product of the Sixties, and I've always been interested in how old things get used and reused. I believe that throwing resources away is outrageous. I learned this from my parents and my grandfather. I got into recycling becauses I was interested in collecting and reusing materials, and I wanted to do something environmental and make a profit at it.

I started out in the recycling business in the early 1970s going door-to-door in Santa Monica, Malibu, and Pacific Palisades, California, collecting aluminum, glass, and newspaper. But it soon became clear to me that collecting recyclables wasn't enough. As more and more people jumped on the recycling bandwagon and the collected materials began piling up, I realized that without market development and new products, recycling was never going to be economically viable for me or for anyone else.

It was time to focus my energies on the economics of processing, manufacturing, and creating new products and markets for all the post-consumer materials being collected across the country. I wanted to see changes made in commercial, industrial, and consumer preferences that would guarantee market demand for goods made from recovered recyclables. One of my market development focuses was the construction industry, because it uses such huge volumes of materials. This tied into my personal interest in creating and living in a sustainable environment.

Working with the construction industry to achieve a sustainable environment makes sense from all standpoints. Good construction is about quality, durability, and longevity. It's about environmental consciousness, energy-saving design, non-toxic materials, and using efficient techniques to construct more cost-effective buildings.

I was thrilled when I was offered the chance in the early 1990s to do a complete build-out in a sustainably designed office, in a high-rise building in downtown Los Angeles. This was my opportunity to prove that "building green" doesn't have to cost more. I was given free rein to apply all the sustainable design principles I wanted to. I focused on energy, construction, accessories, and equipment.

Energy can easily amount to one-third of a commercial building's operating expenses. Here are some of the things we did to reduce energy consumption in this office:

- *Lighting:* The high-output electronic lighting system provides 30 percent more light than standard systems, while still saving 10 to 15 percent in energy costs. These lights are compatible with most other systems, making them ideal for retro-fitting. Also, when operated at high frequency, the lamps become even more efficient, providing up to 40 percent energy savings.

- *Refrigerator:* The refrigerator is energy-efficient and ozone-friendly. It was competitively priced with standard models, but costs an average of only $47 a year to operate; a standard model costs about $110 a year.

- *Office equipment:* All the office equipment, including the photocopier, fax machine, computers, coffee maker, and microwave, are energy-efficient models produced by major manufacturers and available to the general public.

In the construction area, we used the following recycled or reused products:

- *Drywall:* The gypsum-board drywall inside the office is made from 100 percent recycled paper, with some additives like starch and foam.

- *Steel studs:* The steel construction supports are made from 67 percent post-consumer steel, created from a meld of old cars, mattress springs, barbecues, and other scrap metal.

- *Carpet:* The carpet is made from PET plastic soda bottles and the pad is made from recycled tires. Approximately 36 two-liter bottles make a square yard of carpeting. This PET carpet cost $6 per square yard less than standard carpeting.

- *Ceiling panels:* The fiber and wood fiber ceiling panels are made from approximately 85 percent post-consumer industrial content, including a waste product of steel production called slag and a cellulose fiber made from recycled newsprint.

We focused on the "reuse" part of the "reduce, reuse, recycle" equation for some of the accessories, furniture, and equipment. The following items in the office were made from deconstructed building materials from Hollywood movie sets. Needless to say, everyone found these to be the most interesting things in the project!

- Bookshelves and hall credenza, from *Clear and Present Danger*

- Plant box stands, *Dracula, Dead and Loving It*

- Lobby credenza and computer desk, *Speechless*

- Kitchen cabinets, *Dracula, Dead and Loving It*, *Clear and Present Danger*, and *The Little Rascals*

- Conference room cabinet and lobby armchair, *Apollo 13*

- Lunch counter and bar stools, *Batman Forever* and *Congo*

- Log cabinet, made with logs from *On Deadly Ground* and cedar from a Volkswagen commercial

Another interesting aspect of the project is the conference room table. It was made from 100 percent post-consumer cardboard and brown paper bags without using toxic resins or solvents. The materials were turned into pulp, then pressed into panels that are incredibly strong and lightweight. During the office's open house, we had several people test its load-bearing ability by sitting on it. I am pleased to report it withstood everyone's weight.

Other eco-friendly design elements included HEPA air filters, an office plant "bio filter," and a water-filtration system. The office plant/bio filter is disguised as a planter and combines activated carbon and other filtering media with living plants and microorganisms to reduce and eliminate odors and pollutants in the air. The filter material traps and holds indoor pollutants. The plant roots and microorganisms living on and around them convert these harmful pollutants into food for the plant. A small fan built into the base of the planter pulls contaminated air through the plant roots and returns the cleaned air through small slits in the planter base. The water system uses a five-stage, ultraviolet, reverse-osmosis water filter that removes all bacteria, contaminants, and fungi.

Once the office was up and running, we stocked only office supplies that were made from recycled content, preferably post-consumer, or sustainable wood products. At the end of the first year, we calculated the office saved about 12 percent by using recycled supplies.

The completion of this office proved several points I think are vitally important in promoting environmental sustainability. First, eco-construction can be cost-effective. In the end, we came in 10 percent under budget. Second, the "look" of the office was as sophisticated as any other office in the building. Third, life-cycle maintenance is less expensive. Working with building management, we calculated that this office suite used 25 percent less energy than other offices.

The construction industry is finally beginning to see the logic of enlightened self-interest—the competitive and financial advantage to be gained by taking environmental issues into account. Consumers need to keep pushing the message of forward-thinking, innovative building solutions that do not compromise the ability of future generations to meet their own needs.

The following suppliers made this office project a reality: American Hemp; Armstrong; Citiscape; Domtar Gypsum; ECO Systems 2000; FM Water Conditioning; Gordon Floor Coverings; Gridcore; Honeywell; Jules Seltzer Associates; Natural Solutions; Real Goods, Inc.; Rising Star Futons; Spin-offs; System Solutions; and Treeco.

Advanced
Green Building

Pliny Fisk III, Co-director

Center for Maximum Potential Building Systems
8604 F.M. 969
Austin, TX 78724
www.cmpbs.org

The development and promotion of advanced green building is an ongoing focus of the Center for Maximum Potential Building Systems (CMPBS), located on the outskirts of Austin, Texas. Public demonstrations of Advanced Green Building take place in the Center's buildings, where we live and work. These buildings grew out of our work of over 25 years to understand the relationship between people's social needs and the regional ecological parameters within which those needs are met. All of our projects are inquiries into the mechanics of creating environmentally, economically, and humanly responsive buildings. We welcome readers to further explore the physical and theoretical premises of the CMPBS.

In 1989, the CMPBS and the City of Austin founded the Green Builder Program, the first municipal program of its kind in the world. The program has been a significant springboard for our thinking on a public policy level, and it was the only U.S. environmental program recognized at the 1992 Rio Earth Summit. Subsequent research funded by federal and local agencies, the State of Texas, and private foundations as well as considerable material donations from businesses has allowed us to continue our work.

Advanced Green Building assumes the basis of ecological design is a systemic environmental, economic, and spatial understanding. It is also predicated on a gradual and fundamental reorganization of how society handles the four essential flows of any building process: information, money, energy, and materials. These flows are in turn subject to ecological parameters, including the boundaries within which they perform, a life-cycle balance between the source and resourcing of each flow, and synchronicity of flows. Studying Advanced Green Building made it clear to us that human systems must change from hierarchical and centralized to distributed, self-organizing, and regionalized. Multiple feedback loops are essential to guide and balance these systems over time.

In order to design sustainable buildings in today's marketplace, we must make a quantum leap in our ability to evaluate products. We must be able to evaluate materials and building processes in their capacity to work together as successfully as past indigenous builders did with nature. This is not a simple process, nor is it intuitive. The human system has become so complex that there are hundreds and even thousands of processes embedded in every product. This surfeit of upstream ingredients and processes leaves little capacity for nature to make up for our lack of knowledge of the ecological conditions within which these products are placed. Thus, a new understanding of the design and specification processes is required.

Current information on green building is either too general, too difficult to obtain, or does not provide enough data. Additionally, the flow of information is becoming more complex—it is more immediate (by virtue of the Internet), multidimensional (encompassing the environmental and employment impact of products), and particular to specific places. BaselineGreen, a tool developed by the Center, manages all these information flows to evaluate the environmental and economic bottom line from which green building specification decisions can be made. The tool represents information on the material, geographic position, energy, and economic flows within over 12 million businesses in the U.S. and displays each industry's environmental impacts, including greenhouse gases, air pollutants, and toxic releases. The procedure is unique in correlating building specification categories to environmental and economic protocols developed through benchmarked and peer-reviewed procedures. Further developments, pending additional funding, will enable BaselineGreen to assess specification decisions over a product or material's entire life cycle, including longevity and disassembly impact.

Just as we design for energy balance within a passive solar building, adjusting inputs of solar radiation and outputs of heat to create constant temperature, so too can we achieve balances of water, air, and materials, to name just a few. BaselineGreen describes these problems of balance as hierarchical decision-making procedures by identifying impacts for a specific building type. With this tool, we can examine a typical building—a single-family home, for example— and provide such information as where the most environmental impact exists.

This data is in no way a substitute for understanding human relations, specific ecological contexts or the technological know-how in a particular location but merely an indicator of systemic relationships. A building can then be seen as a fractal of the four essential flows (information, currency, energy, and materials) that support a region's industrial and natural ecology. There are different scales at which these flows must be balanced, from a building to its site boundary to the larger region.

The relationship between flow balance and boundaries can provide perspective on the global impact of human activities. For example, the United States requires 20 times its land area to balance the amount of carbon dioxide we produce. Concerns about generating greenhouse gases like carbon dioxide should permeate decisions at almost all scales. We find that each site location has its own unique resources that can contribute to balancing these flows. How we build, even the smallest detail, has profound implications for the planning of a whole region, even the flow of financial capital. Slowing resource rather than balancing it merely delays the inevitability of a whole system failure.

The responsibility for guiding the future rests squarely in our own hands. But we must have adequate tools to work with. Admitting the need to assess the complex interdependencies of cultural, ecological, and economic systems is an important first step towards sustainable design. Eventually, tools like BaselineGreen will raise the standard of specification decisions by enabling architects to evaluate the impact of a building's entire life cycle. Such information cannot replace the need to understand the human relations, specific ecological contexts, or technological capacities of a particular site's context. But making the full spectrum of these invisible yet interdependent systems visible may very well be the key to sustainable design's future.

—∞∞∞—

SECTION 6:

RESOURCES

Wood From Responsible Sources

F. David T. Arens, Director of Marketing

Forest Stewardship Council U.S.
1134 29th Street NW
Washington, DC 20007
www.fscus.org

Admirers of sustainable design took notice recently of the completion of Oberlin College's $6.6 million Joseph Lewis Center for Environmental Studies. Considered by some a model for the application of sustainable design principles, the Lewis Center, a 14,000-square-foot complex set on two-and-a-half acres of the college's Oberlin, Ohio, campus, consists of a two-story rectangular building for classrooms and offices, a smaller structure for an auditorium, and a sunlight-powered wastewater recycling system. The facility also features photovoltaic cells on the roof to convert sunlight into electricity, pesticide-free orchards and gardens around the buildings, a pond and wetland to retain and purify runoff, recyclable flooring and carpeting, and windows and an atrium designed to maximize natural light.

There is also another, more subtle aspect to the Lewis Center's sustainable design. The wood used in its glue-laminated beams, roof deck, interior trim, and auditorium seating comes from responsibly managed forests, forests that adhere to the rules of the Forest Stewardship Council.

The Forest Stewardship Council (FSC) is an independent international non-profit organization that sets standards for well-managed forests. Using the FSC's Principles and Criteria for Forest Management as a major accounting firm might use Generally Accepted Accounting Principles to audit a company's finances, FSC-accredited certification organizations around the world work to verify that timber companies meet its guidelines. As the Introduction to the Principles and Criteria signals, though, the FSC imagines the best forestry to be something more than numbers on a page.

It is widely accepted that forest resources and associated lands should be managed to meet the social, economic, ecological, cultural, and spiritual needs of present and future generations. Furthermore, growing public awareness of forest destruction and degradation has led consumers to demand that their purchases of wood and other forest products will not contribute to this destruction but rather help to secure forest resources for the future.

The FSC defines responsible forestry as a balanced ethos, one that, at once, includes the natural, the social, and the industrial. If this framework is applied successfully, the FSC sees that we can simultaneously conserve forests as landscapes, maintain social structures tied to forests, and preserve forests as an economic resource. But the FSC does not expect that an industry as large and entrenched as the wood products industry will change on the strength of good intentions alone. The Principles and Criteria use a carrot, rather than a stick, to reach the desired end. Harnessing the "growing public awareness of forest degradation," the FSC allows finished products made with wood from responsible sources to carry the FSC's logo, a seal of approval that major U.S. and European home improvement retailers such as The Home Depot and Britain's B&Q now prefer in their purchasing.

Wood from responsibly managed forests, often known in the trade as "certified" wood, is a recent and, potentially, philosophically unique component of sustainable design. Unlike many sustainable design features, certified wood does not, in and of itself, stand out as part of an alternative aesthetic. It does not appear to be any different from its undocumented counterparts, which means that a critic of a designer's work cannot directly access the sensibilities at play.

Though subtle, certified wood's place in sustainable design is significant. At one level, a designer's decision to include certified wood in a project is roughly parallel to a consumer's: both use their market-making power to encourage positive cultural change with enticement rather than sanction. One might anticipate, though, that an architect's stake in forests ought to be a fair bit greater than a consumer's, for at least three reasons. Since an architect's productive aim is to plan for the benefit of many, she serves as an influential intermediary who can establish and sustain trends of many sorts. And since wood is one of the primary structural building materials, any effort to make sure that there is an ongoing, long-term supply of it strikes many in the community as good common sense. Yet the strongest bonds become visible when one considers the historically significant role that the architectural community has played in building awareness of and preserving aesthetics. The movement toward responsible forestry, and especially the role that this movement plays in preserving the beauty and integrity of a natural landscape, is in keeping with the architectural world's more established efforts to preserve significant structures. Incorporating wood from responsible sources allows designers (and those for whom they design) to help preserve one aesthetic—that of the natural forest—while they work to create a lasting one of their own.

Certified wood helped make Oberlin's sustainable design complete. Nancy Orr, president of Oberlin College, noted, "In green design, it's important to pay attention to sourcing of materials. We had to have wood representative of sustainable practices, and we wanted to make sure that the project caused no ugliness, human or ecological." Along with the visible improvements to quality of life that any sustainable design brings, one with responsible wood products includes the assurance that our natural world (and the quality that it adds to our lives when we are not inside) will remain.

To learn more about wood from responsible sources in the U.S. or the FSC's Principles and Criteria for Forest Management, please visit the Web sites of the Certified Forest Products Council (www.certifiedwood.org), the Forest Stewardship Council U.S. (www.fscus.org), or the FSC's certifiers in the U.S., SmartWood (www.smartwood.org) and Scientific Certification Systems (www.scs1.com).

———∞∞∞———

Conservation-Based Lending at a Community Development Bank

Laurie Landeros, EcoDeposits Program,
Steve Gutmann, Credit Analyst,
and Kathleen Sayce, Bank Scientist

ShoreBank Pacific
P.O. Box 400
Ilwaco, WA 98624
www.eco-bank.com

S horeBank Pacific is a community development bank that was established to support the conservation economy in the Pacific Northwest rainforest bioregion, which extends west of the Cascades from Northern California to Alaska. The bank provides services in financing and financial planning, energy and materials-use efficiency, community health, and habitat restoration.

The bank is a federally regulated, FDIC-insured institution, chartered in Washington State, and has close ties to South Shore Bank in Chicago. South Shore Bank pioneered social equity in lending to minorities, women, and poor communities more than 25 years ago, and led the nation in developing community reinvestment legislation. ShoreBank Pacific is a natural outgrowth of this movement, with a focus not only on social equity, but also on conservation-based business.

The Bank actively directs its lending activities to support conservation and restoration of the environment, sustainable economic growth, and economic vitality, including: loans to small businesses, particularly those that are prepared to adopt and use conservation-based development plans and to measure environmental impacts and cost savings; loans that facilitate the development and improvement of low- and moderate-income housing, community services, job creation, and opportunities for small businesses and entrepreneurs; and loans that result in waste reduction, energy efficiency, materials reuse, and the use of sustainably produced materials.

We are often asked about "screens," the measures most lending institutions use to decide which categories of and which specific businesses to consider as clients. ShoreBank Pacific does not use screens. Our philosophy is that any business or household can be run more economically, be remodeled to be more efficient in materials and energy use, and have its processes redesigned to cost less to run. While there are a few types of business where it might be difficult to make improvements, such as mining operations, most businesses show moderate to major increases in efficiency with a reasonable amount of effort.

We are also asked what we tell customers to do to achieve these goals. The answer: The bank does not tell anyone to do anything; instead, we suggest changes that may alter a company's future use of energy and materials, changes that will directly impact the financial bottom line. For example, a local resort was purchasing additional property, which contained several existing buildings. We suggested that the 100-year flood line be reevaluated, as it cut across the property. When this was done, the buildings were discovered to be above the flood line. This finding led to a reduction in insurance costs of more than 75 percent. The new annual insurance fee plus the cost of the evaluation was less than the old fee, saving money in the first year.

We made a loan recently to the Open Meadow Alternative School, a unique institution in the St. Johns neighborhood of Portland, Oregon. For nearly 30 years Open Meadow has offered an array of educational experiences that recognize and support life beyond the classroom. The Youth Employment and Empowerment Project (YEEP) and Corps Restoring the Urban Environment (CRUE) are two such programs at Open Meadow. YEEP offers young people positive alternatives to gang lifestyles by providing employment opportunities and job training. Students typically work with adults as interns or apprentices, learning about the world of work while earning income to enable them to become self-sufficient. CRUE uses out-of-classroom job sites instead of the traditional desks-and-chairs environment. Students earn credits by working on ecological restoration, Geographic Information Systems computer mapping, and social service projects. CRUE also assists students in finding internships to pursue their special areas of interest. Open Meadow students have recently done internships with the Oregon Zoo, Oregon Museum of Science and Industry, *Willamette Week* newspaper, Doernbecher Children's Hospital, and Emanuel Hospital.

The bank works with business owners to incorporate energy efficiency features into buildings and operations, and to inform them about tax savings and loan options. When money is spent on power, most of that money immediately leaves the community. Reducing energy costs of all types (gasoline, electricity, natural gas, coal, etc.) results in savings that are more likely to be redirected locally. It is also cheaper for utilities to conserve than to create new power-generation capacity. The local public utility offers no-interest loans to cover energy efficiency alterations to homes and businesses; across the river in Oregon, the state offers business tax credits for spending on energy efficiency.

Another EcoDeposits success story sits at the mouth of the Columbia River, in Astir, Oregon. For more than 10 years, a 16-acre site there stood desolate behind a chain-link fence. Once a plywood mill with its own log sorting pond and veneer peeling and gluing lines, it had become a classic brownfield site, left behind when the business closed shop. Petroleum products coated the surface of the four-acre pond and soaked the ground; PCBs were concentrated in several areas.

ShoreBank Enterprise Pacific (SEP), our non-profit affiliate, was willing to take a risk on the site to help clean it up. The City of Astoria's perseverance in pursuing remediation attracted SEP's participation with a $750,000 commitment to cost-share with the Oregon Department of Environmental Quality (DEQ) to clean up the old mill site to acceptable state standards. DEQ found money in a Federal fund to pay most of the $2 million-plus cost outright. Contaminated soil was burned on-site to remove oil and PCBs. Oil was scooped off the water and burned. Once this was done, the site wasn't pristine, but it was safe for commercial and residential use.

The town proposed mixed use—a combination of residential and commercial buildings—for the valuable waterfront property. An innovative developer, Art DeMuro of Venerable Properties, Inc., stepped forward and was awarded the development contract by the city. DeMuro turned to ShoreBank Pacific to help bring his vision of green development and historic restoration to reality. Mill Pond Village was designed in keeping with the historic character and eclectic architecture of Astoria. The master plan includes narrow streets, small lots with front porches, and easy walking access. Green building design guidelines that highlight efficient resource use result in cost-effective, comfortable homes that blend into the larger community.

An elegant pergola now stands at the edge of a tranquil tidal pond, where oil once crusted the surface and old logging machinery lay submerged in its depths. Tracks of deer, raccoon, and great blue heron dot the small tidal beaches, and plant life has returned: iris, bulrush, soft rush, Queen Anne's lace. What was once a polluted mill site is now an idyllic setting for homes and offices. "Mill Pond Village would not have happened without the contributions of a few key players," DeMuro noted in a recent interview. "Near the top of that list is ShoreBank Pacific. The Bank's out-of-the-box approach and willingness to support environmentally sensitive redevelopment made financing of this innovative project possible."

EcoDeposits provides the support for ShoreBank Pacific's conservation-based lending program. When depositors bring their savings to ShoreBank Pacific, those savings are invested in loans to help the local conservation economy. We offer the standard range of savings instruments to depositors at competitive interest rates. All ShoreBank accounts are FDIC insured up to $100,000. The bank raises deposits in North America and overseas, and currently has depositors in over 40 states and seven foreign countries. Our work would not be possible without the vision and will of our depositors to invest in the future.

How a Mortgage Can Make a Difference

Donna Liu, Staff Policy Analyst

Natural Resources Defense Council
71 Stevenson Street, #1825
San Francisco, CA 94105
www.nrdc.org

You want to buy a house but your bank says you don't qualify for a loan.

Chances are your bank is using an antiquated but well-established method of determining whether you can responsibly assume a monthly mortgage payment. For decades the private lending community has recognized an increased risk when a consumer pays more than 28% of their gross household income toward a mortgage payment. This payment covers the principal, interest, taxes, and insurance of a home loan over either an adjustable or fixed length of time. Called the "front end ratio", this 28% rule is applied to all applicant households regardless of where the house or condo is located. A 36% "back-end ratio" caps the amount of mortgage payment and additional debt such as student loans and credit cards.

Enter the Location Efficient Mortgage (a service mark of the Institute for Location Efficiency). This mortgage recognizes the transportation-related cost savings of living in a compact community with transit access and retail uses. The intent of the mortgage is to allow homebuyers to capitalize on these savings by qualifying for a higher loan amount than they would if buying in a less compact or low-density area. The result is increased ratios and thus a higher loan amount for the urban homebuyer.

For areas in which the mortgage is available, lenders are now factoring into their decision-making how location can positively influence the loan risk. As one lender put it, "The research behind this mortgage scientifically justifies what we have always intuitively known."

The Research

The Natural Resources Defense Council partnered with the Surface Transportation Policy Project and the Center for Neighborhood Technology to research the relationship between the physical characteristics of a neighborhood and personal transportation behavior for three regions: San Francisco, Chicago, and Los Angeles. Building upon a 1994 study sponsored by NRDC, the partners developed a methodology to predict the average number of cars owned and miles driven by households based on the physical factors of a community. These factors include density, transit access, and pedestrian friendliness of the neighborhood. Additional variables found to be statistically relevant were household income and household size. The variables were tested to show how much they collectively influence household transportation expenses. Augmented with data from the Federal Highway Administration (FHWA), the partners are now able to conservatively determine how much a household will spend on transportation.

Building Sustainable Communities

As the United States enjoys its current economic boom and our metropolitan centers grow with jobs and workers, the suburbs surrounding these urban cores are fanning out and engulfing vast tracts of open land. Helping increase suburban demand is how mortgage lenders in the U.S. have applied loan requirements to urban and suburban homebuyers in similar fashion, without examining how place affects the homebuyer's ability to meet their loan repayment.

These 28%/36% ratio restrictions have very success-fully fueled the exodus of would-be urban homebuyers into lower-priced areas where banks can approve their loan. These lower-priced communities generally are the outlying suburbs where land and development fees are cheaper. While we watch and wait, these low-density communities become ever more expan-sive and place strains on water supplies and open space; increase the demand for publicly funded highway infrastructure; spur native wildlife out of their own habitat; and contribute to a transportation pattern that increases auto use and air pollution. The irony is that transportation expenses increase the farther out from the metropolitan core a household moves, increasing overall household expenses, but it wasn't until the Location Efficient Mortgage that the lending community started to understand how location affects a household's transportation needs.

How the Location Efficient Mortgage Works

When comparing how much an urban household spends on transportation versus a household in the lowest-density quartile of the region, the monetary difference is called the Location Efficient Value (LEV). The level of impact that the Location Efficient Mortgage has on someone buying a home depends on the Location Efficient Value that accrues to a household based on location, income, and household size.

For example, if a household has $200/month in LEV, this is added onto the household's qualifying income, boosting the amount of a mortgage for which they can qualify. Over a 30-year mortgage, this may mean a $50,000 increase in housing price.

With the Location Efficient Mortgage, the new front-end ratio for total housing payment is increased to 39% of gross income, or 35% of income including the LEV; and 49% including long-term debt or 45% calculated with the LEV. Consumers must meet all ratio tests. The 11% front-end differential over a 30-year-loan can mean tens of thousands of additional dollars for which a household can qualify.

Partnerships

In 1996 NRDC and its project partners approached Fannie Mae, the nation's largest source of mortgage funds, to engage them as a partner in making Location Efficient Mortgages a reality. Working with Fannie Mae is imperative as they buy billions of dollars in housing debt from retail banks and other mortgage financing institutions. Without the presence of a government-sponsored enterprise like Fannie Mae, lenders are not as willing to take on the risk of an innovative but untested underwriting product like the Location Efficient Mortgage. It should be noted that this is not just about loan risk. Banks incur thousands of dollars in implementing new programs through system changes, personnel training and marketing efforts. Engaging on a new product with a major partner improves the likelihood that the product will be sustainable in the marketplace. Fannie Mae subsequently approved a two-year, $127 million test of the Location Efficient Mortgage for four areas: the cities of Chicago and Seattle, Los Angeles and Orange Counties, and the nine-county San Francisco Bay Area.

One question facing the partners was how to deliver LEVs to the originating lender. A solution devised for Seattle, Chicago, and Los Angeles County uses Web-based maps found at www.locationefficiency.com.

Essentially, any user can navigate through the Web site and find their community of interest at the travel analysis zone (TAZ) level, which can be nearly identical to a census tract. From there, with inputs of household income, available down payment, interest rate, and household size, the user sees how much of a home they can purchase in this neighborhood. The site also allows the user to compare maximum loan amounts between the Location Efficient Mortgage and the conventional lending formula.

The Location Efficient Mortgage Versus Other Mortgage Products

There are dozens of mortgage designs from which a lucky borrower can choose. For those borrowers who find themselves hoping to live in an urban environment but just shy of qualifying for a standard loan, this unique underwriting structure is the solution to their particular dilemma. The research partners are pleased that the mortgage is a market-based product, meaning that there are no subsidies attached, no special pools of public money involved, and no income restriction. The success of the Location Efficient Mortgage is correlated to the demand for housing in compact, transit-served neighborhoods. We hope that with this product available in the marketplace consumers will choose more livable communities over living on the urban fringe.

The Commercial High Performance Buildings Project

Michael J. Crosbie, Associate, and
William José Higgins, Architect

Steven Winter Associates, Inc.
50 Washington Street
Norwalk, CT 06854
www.swinter.com

The Commercial High Performance Buildings project is part of the U.S. Department of Energy's (DOE) Commercial Whole-Building Roadmapping initiative. The purpose of the program is to demonstrate and publicize innovative concepts using comprehensive systems engineering approaches that increase the quality and efficiency of commercial buildings while reducing their costs and environmental impacts. (According to Energy Information Administration estimates, commercial buildings use approximately one-sixth of all the energy in this country.) The idea of looking at a building as an interrelated system grew out of the recognition that past research into isolated building components did not take into account how individual systems affect other systems. For example, a building that uses extensive daylighting techniques will reduce the amount of heat given off by light fixtures, thus allowing a smaller air-conditioning system to be installed. Studies that focused on, for example, HVAC efficiency would have missed this relationship.

The High Performance Building project is made up of a core advisory group, which will be involved throughout the life of the project, as well as building-specific satellite groups. The core group is composed of a wide range of professionals in the architecture, engineering, construction, materials manufacturing, government, and publishing fields. The project's current activities focus on publicizing noteworthy commercial buildings in the media, in live presentations at conferences, and on the Internet, at www.eren.doe.gov/buildings/highperformance.

One of the program's first priorities was to assemble a database of high performance buildings that will be available through the Web site and publicized in a variety of forums. The database currently details some 100 buildings from around the country that exhibit high performance qualities such as energy efficiency, environmental sustainability, superior quality, and cost effectiveness. Later activities will include contributing to the design, construction, and evaluation of exemplary commercial buildings through early participation in the development process.

What is a High Performance Building?

No, high performance buildings don't go from zero to 60 miles per hour in five seconds. An abbreviated definition for "high performance buildings" could be those that are energy efficient, have low short- and long-term costs, are healthy for their occupants, and have a low impact on the environment.

Achieving these goals, however, involves more than simply meeting cost and efficiency requirements. A high performance building design is an all-inclusive philosophy. First, there must be a team approach to the design. This design team should include not only the architects, engineers, and owners, but also the future building occupants and specialists in indoor air quality, materials, energy, costs, etc. With so many parties involved, reaching consensus can be difficult; one solution is to have a peer review early in the design process, during which the experts and other people involved in the project get together for a one-day or two-day critique of the preliminary design. Second, regarding design, the interaction of the whole building structure, its systems, and its context should be considered. This whole building philosophy should include site issues, energy, materials, indoor air quality, indoor environmental quality, and resources, and how they are all interrelated. Third, a high performance building considers how the facility will perform over the long term. The life-cycle maintenance costs, durability, energy usage, and effect on the occupants and the environment must all be analyzed.

The Benefits of High Performance Buildings

High performance buildings have many potential benefits over conventional ones for the owner, occupants, and the environment. Long-term mainte-nance costs and annual energy costs are lower. Building occupants and visitors enjoy a healthier interior environment. Worker productivity can improve with better lighting and a more comfortable indoor atmosphere. A high performance building can help attract tenants. The building will be a better neighbor and will have fewer negative impacts on the natural environment.

Paths to High Performance Buildings

One way to help define a high performance building is to use a building rating system such as the U.S. Green Building Council's LEED (Leadership in Energy and Environmental Design) Green Building Rating System. LEED is a comprehensive rating system that helps the designer wade through the numerous issues involved in creating a high perfor-mance whole building. LEED focuses on sustainable sites, water efficiency and energy efficiency, materials and resources, and indoor environmental quality.

Another helpful program is EPA's Energy Star label for buildings, which covers energy consumption and some of the indoor environment. It provides a Web-based benchmarking tool that can show where a building stands in comparison to similar buildings nationwide. The user inputs the building's physical attributes, operating characteristics, and energy consumption and then receives a score of 0 to 100. A score of 75 means that the building is more efficient than 75 percent of similar buildings in the U.S. and is thus entitled to the Energy Star label.

The Federal Energy Management Program (FEMP) is a DOE program for federal buildings to reduce energy and water use, manage utility costs, and promote renewable energy. The many FEMP resources include analytical software tools, a building commissioning guide, descriptions of federal "greening" projects, renewable energy information, the SAVEnergy Program, and water conservation information.

How to Participate

The first way to participate in the Commercial High Performance Buildings program is to alert the project management team, Steven Winter Associates, about high performance buildings that you have been involved with. Another is to present proposed high performance buildings, early in the planning stage, to Steven Winters Associates in order to obtain technical support. Finally, architects and designers can join the U.S. Green Building Council (www.usgbc.org) and become involved in the LEED Green Building Rating System, which will help clarify the whole building design approach and help create valuable tools for creating high performance buildings.

The AIA's Sustainability Resolution

Sara Malone, Editor

The American Institute of Architects
1735 New York Avenue NW
Washington, DC 20006
www.aiaonline.com

Architects are pivotal to the creation of a sustainable society, one that can extend far into the future without exhausting its key resources. The American Institute of Architects has long recognized the effect of architecture on the environment, and it reconfirmed its commitment to sustainability at its 2000 Convention in Philadelphia.

During the convention, members overwhelmingly approved a resolution to "acknowledge sustainable design as the basis of quality design and responsible practice for AIA architects and, therefore, to integrate sustainable design into AIA practices and procedures."

In other words, said Sandra Mendler, AIA, chair of the AIA's Committee on the Environment (COTE), "sustainability is fundamental to quality design, not just an optional niche market."

The resolution clarified goals long held by the AIA, which since the 1980s has urged architects to place environmental and social sustainability at the core of their practices. It has supported this mission through initiatives such as The Greening of Federal Facilities, a 1993 feasibility study on improving energy efficiency; and the Environmental Resource Guide (ERG), published in 1992 and 1996 in partnership with the Environmental Protection Agency and John Wiley & Sons.

In addition to strategic alliances with organizations such as the Green Building Council and the American Solar Energy Society, COTE compiles the annual Earth Day Top 10 list of green architecture, hosts biannual conferences on sustainability, and participates in charrettes.

One of the AIA Committee on the Environment's top initiatives for 2000 is the Next Generation Design Resources guide, currently under development. The guide will clarify the architect's role, engage in research to fill in information holes, and document the integrated design process and successful case studies. "As leaders of our profession, we should be articulating what we need in terms of a research agenda to keep us evolving and moving into the future," said Mendler. "[The guide will] let us identify where our gaps are in our knowledge, and go about filling in those gaps and the knowledge."

COTE also is focusing on architectural education. This year it is hosting a round-table discussion with deans of architecture schools and leading experts in sustainable design to determine how to shift sustainability from peripheral course work into the core of the curriculum. Among other things, COTE hopes to establish, over the next three years, three to five programs that will serve as models for architectural schools interested in focusing on sustainability.

The resolution passed at AIA's 2000 convention draws on efforts such as these to make architects accountable for their environmental impact. "We of necessity are some of the worst offenders," observed John Corkill, AIA, chair of the AIA's Professional Interest Area Executive Committee and a supporter of the resolution. "We draw up a building and the next thing you know here come the bulldozers and down go the trees, and off fly the birds, and the turtles get squashed. It's just carnage out there—we in the building industry have a very special need to watch ourselves, to mind our Ps and Qs."

Another issue of the resolution involves the AIA's advocacy role. Corkill used the fight against sick building syndrome as an example, which code writers at

American Society of Heating, Refridgerating & Air-Conditioning Engineers, Inc. addressed by requiring that 20 cubic feet of fresh air per minute per person be brought into a building. "You're saying that if this building were located say in the Midwest, where it's 20 below zero, we're going in one hour to take in 240,000 cubic feet of subzero air, and then warm it up to 70 degrees?" asked Corkill. The energy costs would bankrupt the outfit, he added. The AIA, in its advocating position, could work with code writers to prevent such unintentionally harmful results.

The resolution also calls for the inclusion of sustainability into AIA contract documents, which will increase the likelihood that buildings that do not harm the environment will get built. Among the documents that will see a change in language are the architect-owner-contractor agreements and the Handbook of Professional Practice. COTE is also working to make sustainability a more prominent part of the AIA's continuing education program.

With this resolution, the AIA's position on sustainability extends far beyond environmental effects related to materials. "One of the things we've said as a committee," noted Mendler, "is that with sustainable design there's been too much focus on building technology. What we need now is to look holistically at land use, planning, and community issues."

Is There a
New Current
of Sustainability?

Deborah Dunning, Director

The International Design Center for the Environment
15 T. W. Alexander Drive
Research Triangle Park, NC 27709
www.idce.org

Is there a current in America strong enough to thrust the "sustainability movement" into mainstream design, building, and furnishing within this decade?

Five professionals active in architecture, business, environmental management, and technology think so. Gail Lindsey, Linda Rimer, Mark Benson Stuart Hart, and I have created a non-profit organization, the International Design Center for the Environment, or IDCE, to develop additional resources for this effort. We have embarked on this venture with both humility and hope. Our humility is based on our recognition of how much there is to know in the emerging field of sustainability. Our hope comes from sensing that there are a great many potential partners out there — individuals as well as agencies and institutions — willing to join together and develop the new resources needed for the mainstreaming of sustainability in America.

IDCE Opened in September of 1999 in Research Triangle Park, North Carolina. Its mission is to strengthen and expand market demands for sustainable practices in the design and manufacture of building materials and furnishings. To further these goals, we recently commissioned four MBA students at the University of North Carolina to conduct market surveys of several professional groups to determine what resource gaps exist and to strategize about filling those gaps.

The research findings have been our guide. They tell us that there is a lack of clear, commonly accepted measures for the performance of building materials and furnishings that could give consumers information (or third-party verification) of the level of environmental responsibility of the products available in the marketplace. There is no comprehensive source of easily accessible information, such as a Web site, that could provide professionals with all of the available material on sustainable materials, products, and technologies in succinct, user-friendly form. There is a lack of cost-effective and time-efficient education programs on sustainable practices. And economic incentives are needed to make sustainable products and technologies economically viable until the market for them matures.

Working with UNC students' survey results, IDCE has developed its goals for the next 10 years, recognizing that they can be achieved only by working in partnership with other like-minded agencies, companies, and groups. The founders hope that a number of organizations will choose to partner with us in finding ways to implement the following five goals, together producing the best possible new resources:

Goal One: Promote a well-researched set of benchmark metrics for building materials and furnishings.

Our research found that 93 percent of the participants in the market survey believe development of a comprehensive eco-label is important or very important. IDCE will develop its own label for building materials and furnishings, using the UL (Underwriters Laboratories) label as a model and following the processes established by The National Institute of Standards and Technologies.

Some existing labels may be encompassed in this comprehensive label, such as those developed by Athena, Climate Wise, EPP, Forest Stewardship Council, and others. The goal is to achieve standards for all materials used in a given product and which factor in a full life-cycle analysis of it. The ultimate aim is to have a system of standards helpful to manufacturers, purchasers, and end users alike for building materials, furniture, and furnishings.

Goal Two: Provide technology assistance to professionals and manufacturers, focusing on new applications of sustainable materials.

The Internet has clearly been a boon for the sustainable design community. Noting that 85 percent of the survey respondents already use the Internet, and that most believe additional electronic resources on sustainability are needed, IDCE will collaborate with other non-profits to create a database of the most current information on green building and furnishing technologies, products, and resource professionals. Coupled with purchasing and project management software, this promises to be a powerful tool. Other databases may be included as well, such as one comparing the full life-cycle impact of all of the major materials used in furniture manufacturing. With access to this tool, manufacturers argue, their industrial designers can more fully incorporate environmental footprint analyses into their materials decisions. As the initial cost for most "green" products is 5 percent (or more) higher than conventional materials, this life-cycle information will provide an important selling point for sustainable design and construction.

Goal Three: Educate professionals and the general public on sustainable practices and products.

Ninety-nine percent of the participants in the market

survey spoke of the value of educational workshops on sustainable resources and technologies. IDCE intends to respond to this need for more educational offerings by developing two series of educational workshops on environmentally responsible choices— one for professionals and a second for the general public. Both will be available on the Web in addition to group presentations at the Sustainable Resources Center, where IDCE will be located permanently, once it opens in the fall of 2001. Topics in the workshops, to be led by Gail Lindsey, will include "Integrated Design for Site, Energy, Materials, Indoor Air Quality and Water"; "Sustainable Design and Development Resources"; "Rating Systems and Other Assessment Tools"; "Green Case Studies"; and "Focusing on Your Firm's Current Projects."

Additionally, IDCE plans to create a 50,000- to 80,000-square-foot, year-round Sustainable Products Exhibit Hall within the Resources Center being created in North Carolina. Visitors to the hall will become engaged in learning about sustainable building materials and sustainable furnishings in new, highly experiential ways.

Goal Four: Take a leadership role in developing economic incentives to support the use of sustainable practices.

IDCE intends to form a consortium of non-profits and professional organizations that will communicate to lawmakers the importance of developing Federal incentives to reward sustainable building and furnishing. Our models for this effort are the Federal (and later state) preservation tax credits, initially passed in 1976 and revised in 1986. In the 22 years since their adoption, the credits have stimulated $40 billion in investments in historic properties.

The benefits from these investments have included improved neighborhoods, new jobs, and retained historical resources. Without these tax credits, a great many communities would still be deteriorated, their historic resources wasted rather than recycled.

Goal Five: Model and showcase sustainable practices and products through sustainable community development.

In selecting a location for IDCE's permanent home, the founders focused on placing their headquarters and resource center in a community willing to embrace sustainable development. By drawing on the history of the site chosen—the former White Furniture Company complex near Raleigh-Durham, listed on the National Register of Historic Places— the developers can showcase how preservation and sustainable building technologies can be successfully married. Additionally, this property is situated adjacent to a major rail line used by both Amtrak and the North Carolina Railroad, offering opportunities to develop public transportation to the resource center.

There's a saying that "still waters run deep." There is a new current moving. Don't mistake the frothy effluents of our industrial past for the deep green flow of tomorrow. Once these new resources—and others being developed by the many outstanding agencies and organizations in the U.S. focused to some measure on sustainability—are in place, sustainable design and development will have sufficient force to be mainstream. When together we have achieved this, we will all know not only that we have honored our commitments to ourselves, our families, and our communities, but also that we have honored our country by making America a leader in sustainable design and development, respected for its initiatives and its accomplishments around the globe.

Environmental Building News

Alex Wilson, Executive Editor

Environmental Building News
122 Birge Street, Suite 30
Brattleboro, VT 05301
www.BuildingGreen.com

Like the entire discipline of sustainable architecture, *Environmental Building News* (EBN) grew out of the solar buildings movement of the 1970s. I worked in New Mexico teaching solar greenhouse construction before moving to Vermont to direct the New England Solar Energy Association. I left that position in 1985 to become a freelance author and journalist, building on the expertise I had developed in energy-efficient design and construction practices. In my writing, I drew on my background in biology to weave in environmental topics whenever possible.

The inspiration for EBN came in 1990 when, as a contributing editor to *Architecture* magazine, I wrote an influential article in its award-winning green issue.

In 1991, I hired Nadav Malin, who had been working as a house builder, to develop a training manual for energy-efficient construction practices. The two of us soon began brainstorming a professional newsletter that would offer something new: a forum devoted to environmental issues and buildings.

By the spring of 1992, we had enough of a concept to test at the annual Buildings Conference of the organization I had once directed, which was now called the Northeast Sustainable Energy Association. Thanks to an encouraging response from this core group, *Environmental Building News* was launched in July 1992.

In retrospect, we had a lot to learn! When Nadav and I started the newsletter, we envisioned homebuilders and commercial building contractors as a major part of our audience. During those first few years we learned two important lessons that caused us to reorient our focus towards the design community— and architects in particular. The first lesson was that at least 90 percent of a building's environmental impacts are determined by the design, so the builder really doesn't have that much leverage. After an article in our inaugural issue on protecting trees during construction, we struggled to come up with more topics of direct relevance to builders. Aside from some stuff on construction and demolition waste management, we failed to come up with much, and we now realize that we are really relevant only to builders who are also involved with design aspects of their projects.

The second lesson, which reinforced the conclusions from the first, is that builders don't expect to pay for information. They typically learn what they need to know from free, advertising-laden magazines, from their contacts at the lumber yard, and from their peers at the coffee counter. As a result, getting them to fork over hard cash for a subscriber-supported publication is a tough sell. A flip side to this story is that builders experience the environmental impacts of their work firsthand, at least as far as the local ecosystems on the site are concerned. As a result, the handful of builders who really care about the environment are among our most committed subscribers.

In keeping with our philosophy of providing readers with useful and unbiased information, Nadav and I have continued to seek out important, and often under-reported, environmental topics in the building industry. We try to tackle technically difficult and often thorny topics and provide our readers with a concise and understandable analysis, and with a check-list of recommendations.

In some cases, the conclusions are pretty straightforward. For example, we've written two articles on wood treated with chromated copper arsenate (CCA), which exposed a number of health issues related to its use and looked at significant concerns about disposal; a look at light pollution and the deleterious effect lighting has on the night sky; and an examination of thermal mass and R-values that debunked a number of common myths and clarified the issues that surround this often-misunderstood measure of thermal performance.

Other issues, such as the debates around PVC or the selection of insulation materials, are less clear-cut. In such cases, we do our best to ferret out any less-publicized information, outline the salient points, and generally give our readers the tools to make their own informed decisions. Many subscribers appreciate this approach, but there is always pressure to provide simple conclusions. One of my favorite comments from a reader is: "Enough with all the ecobabble, just give the answers!"

Since those early days we've expanded quite a bit, and added new products to our line-up. We now publish annually a CD-ROM of our archives and a directory of green building products. We co-publish a software tool, the Green Building Advisor, that provides green suggestions customized to a building project, and supports those suggestions with detailed case studies.

The learning curve doesn't seem to be leveling off yet, however. Although we've had a serious Web site since 1996, we've just started to take advantage of the amazing possibilities of the Internet for publishing and connecting all the different types of information that designers need to make green buildings. We're thrilled by the possibilities, but also intimidated by the challenge of making a living in electronic media—a challenge made especially difficult by our reluctance to be supported by advertising. Regardless of the medium, however, it's increasingly clear that green building is a rapidly growing field, and running an information source at the hub of this whirlwind is a role I cherish.

—◦◦◦◦—

GreenClips

Christine Hammer, Consultant and Publisher

GreenClips
3168 Washington Street #6
San Francisco, CA 94115
www.greenclips.com

GreenClips is a free clipping service that summarizes articles on sustainable design, development, and construction from national and international media sources. GreenClips is published via e-mail every two weeks. Each issue contains five to six clips, each of which includes the original publication name, date, page number, and byline. The stories focus on energy and water conservation, environmentally responsible building materials, waste reduction, indoor air quality, and macro urban design issues such as suburban sprawl.

The service currently has over 8,500 e-mail subscribers and is growing at a rate of 80 percent per year. Its target audience is architects, engineers, urban planners, facility managers, builders, university professors and students, environmentalists, government officials, and politicians. GreenClips' brief and concise format is popular with busy professionals.

I regularly scan about 60 publications for stories, including specialty newsletters such as *Environmental Building News*, professional journals like *Architectural Record*, and dailies like *The New York Times*. Since GreenClips started in 1994, the number of sources has increased due to the launch of several new green publications such as *Green@Work*, *Environmental Design & Construction*, and the U.K.'s *Journal of Sustainable Product Design*. The increase in publications is an indication that sustainable design is here to stay.

GreenClips' start, like many ideas, was a convergence of several things. I had just finished my master's of architecture degree at Kansas State University, where I studied the content and format of the American Institute of Architects' Environmental Resource Guide for my thesis. I still use the findings of my research today as a guide to select articles for GreenClips. By 1994, I had assembled a long list of e-mail addresses of friends and colleagues who shared my interest in the impact of design and construction on the environment. And my husband received an e-mail newsdigest, EduPage, which became a model for GreenClips. Reading, especially magazines, has always been a form of relaxation for me. I clip articles routinely and stick them in a folder for later use. All of the above came together in the first issue of GreenClips, which was published in June 1994. The content and format of the first issue was the same as GreenClips today.

My interest in the environment began in high school, at the height of the 1970s oil embargo, during debates with my father over the price of gas and energy conservation. Even though he drove a gas-guzzling car, he was interested in solar energy and scolded me when I didn't turn the lights off. Ironically, the price of gas and energy conservation are still hot issues, especially this summer, as the price of gas jumped above two dollars a gallon. My beliefs are the same as they were in high school. As a culture we continue to be wasteful, and we have developed habits based on the illusion of infinite oil reserves. But we could conserve a lot of energy by being conscious of the consequences of our actions. The intent of GreenClips is to educate the design and construction community about ways we can save energy and generally reduce our impact on the environment. And it does this without using reams of paper.

All back issues of GreenClips are available on our Website::
www.greenclips.com

To subscribe free of charge to GreenClips visit:
http://listserv.energy.wsu.edu/guest/RemoteListSummary/
GreenClips

Building Community

Lynne Elizabeth, Editor

New Village Journal
2000 Center Street, Suite 120
Berkeley, CA 94704
www.newvillage.net

"**R**ebuilders are those who take what other people only talk about and make it the next generation's reality."

—Joan Chittister

Criticism of the ecological and cultural bankruptcies of our civilization is not in itself effective in bringing about change. Focusing solely on problems cannot provide the motivation for true transformation; it polarizes issues, leads to despair, and alienates many who might otherwise embrace better options. Like an unskilled parent, our society has invested vast resources in systems of crisis response, policing, and punishment, a practice that compounds the hardships of people and environments already marginalized by years of exploitation, discrimination, and disinvestment. In contrast, healthier cultures can be built through positive visioning — that is, clarifying a preferred future — and nurturing equitable systems that serve the common good.

New paradigms are not created separately from the old; they evolve, within and from the established culture, arising from the same people and processes that have been declared dysfunctional. One of the dilemmas facing pioneers of cultural evolution is the fragmented nature of knowledge and practice. The multiple facets of community development frequently involve independently operating sets of experts and specialist agencies.

The challenge is to rebuild our culture in integrative ways — ways in which social, economic, and physical infrastructures can be built simultaneously. Embracing this challenge are growing legions of individuals and organizations — community builders — who make it their job to link specialists, foster partnerships among parallel interests, and break down institutional and social barriers to more holistic processes. Growing out of the urban poverty programs of previous decades, the community building movement is shifting the social welfare focus from a community's needs or lacks to focus on the resources it already has, and then mobilizing those resources. (This practice of "asset-mapping" was popularized by John McKnight and John Kretzmann of Northwestern University.) Community building is all the ways we come together to care for the commonwealth. Its prevailing theme is "comprehensiveness," an enlightened approach that incorporates housing, job development and training, child care, health care, spiritual nourishment, and other components of a well-rounded life.

At the movement's core lie myriad community development corporations. Originally small grassroots non-profits, these groups have become the powerful backbone of economic development, affordable housing, and social services in many neighborhoods, leveraging fragmented funding and forging cooperation among disparate agencies as they go. They have in large part taken up the development tasks that government has forsaken. While bureaucracies have been slow to change, these nimble non-governmental organizations are quick to innovate and serve a constantly changing populace. They also lead the way for governmental institutions in the practice of participatory planning, showing cities the benefits of non-hierarchical, bottom-up community building. Community-based development organizations bring to the fore the importance of empowering local citizens and of starting initiatives from within a community.

Increasingly it is being recognized that neighborhood development initiatives are the crucible for sustainable societal change. Village-scale strategies may be employed for reasons that include the following:

- Social capital, the nonmonetary web of human caring that increases a community's well-being and productive potential, is built on the neighborhood level.

- Community-scale development is pivotal to solving problems of profligate sprawling land use, since community-based cultures that value access over mobility and social interchange over material wealth significantly reduce demands on infrastructure and resources.

- Appropriate and community-scale technologies for agriculture, water and sanitation, health care, energy, and construction lessen environmental impacts.

- A renaissance of local enterprise fosters the creativity and artistic expression that have been lost in an industrialized culture.

- Neighborhood-scale and locally owned businesses strengthen local economies, leading to greater self-sufficiency and community health.

- The downsizing of government service agencies and dismantling of welfare programs is increasing the demand for neighborhood-scale, decentralized approaches to serving the needs of poor and middle income populations.

There have been few mechanisms to distill the lessons from recent experience in community building and present them in an engaging format. In response, the non-profit organization Architects/Designers/Planners for Social Responsibility has launched *New Village Journal*. *New Village* makes more broadly accessible the many promising strategies for sustainable community development and renewal that were previously available only to a limited few. It speaks to a diverse audience of practitioners and citizen activists, providing inspiration and real models for the making of compassionate and healthy urban cultures. This semiannual national journal covers such issues as revitalization and local economies, and education for community building.

⎯⎯⎯∞⎯⎯⎯

earth pledge

Corporate Support

Earth Pledge would like to acknowledge and whole-heartedly thank the following sponsors for supporting us in our efforts to promote sustainable architecture: 1 Minute Webcast, 3M, Adimé Internationale, American Hydrotech, Inc., Artemide, Audio Visual Systems, B&B Italia USA, Inc., Balmori Associates, Inc., Benjamin Moore & Co., BP Solar, Bretford Manufacturing, Inc., Carolina Stalite Co., Catalano, Champion Wire, Chronomite Laboratories, Inc., Computer Generated Solutions Inc., Construction Specifiers Institute, Crestron Electronics, Inc., Dornbracht, EarthCam, Inc., Environmental Construction Outfitters, Event Webcasting, Inc., First Smart Sensor, Corp., Flogiston, Franke Kitchen Systems, Freudenberg Building Systems, Inc., Gaggenau USA, Goldman Associates of New York Inc., Hastings Tile & Il Bagno Collection, Hugh

O'Kane Electric Co. LLC, I.G. Federal, IBM, International Association of Lighting Designers, International Brotherhood of Electrical Workers, Local Union #3, Jay R. Smith Manufacturing, Co., Jenn-Air, Lindsley Consultants, Lutron Electronics, Inc., Maytag Corp., Inc., Meazzastone, Metro, Metropolis Magazine, Microsoft Corp., Miele, Inc., Mintec Corp., Mobius 0, New York Fixture Company, Noochee Solutions, Oceanside Glasstile Company, Ron and Eilene Oehl, Pella Corp., Poliform USA, Inc., Pyrolave USA, RCN Telecom, SieMatic Corp., Smart Technologies, Inc., Solar Design Associates, Inc., Sonance, Sterltech, Inc., Stone Source, Sub-Zero, Inc., Toto USA, Umbra,Inc., USM Modular Furniture, Verilux, The Wiremold Company, Wolkow Braker Roofing, Woods & Jaye Sales Co., Zumtobel Staff Lighting.